WORLD DIRECTORS SERIES

Film retains its capacity to beguile, entertain and open up windows onto other cultures like no other medium. Nurtured by the growth of film festivals worldwide and by cinephiles from all continents, a new generation of directors has emerged in this environment over the last few decades.

This new series aims to present and discuss the work of the leading directors from across the world on whom little has been written and whose exciting work merits discussion in an increasingly globalised film culture. Many of these directors have proved to be ambassadors for their national film cultures as well as critics of the societies they represent, dramatising in their work the dilemmas of art that are both national and international, of local relevance and universal appeal.

Written by leading film critics and scholars, each book contains an analysis of the director's works, filmography, bibliography and illustrations. The series will feature film-makers from all continents (including North America), assessing their impact on the art form and their contribution to film culture.

Other Titles in the Series

WORLD DIRECTORS

EMIR KUSTURICA

Dina Iordanova

 Publishing

PN1998.3
.K88
I57
2002x

0419739209

First published in 2002 by the
BRITISH FILM INSTITUTE
21 Stephen Street, London W1T 1LN

The British Film Institute promotes greater understanding of,
and access to, film and moving image culture in the UK.

Design by Ketchup
Cover image: *Underground* (Emir Kusturica, 1995)
Set by D R Bungay Associates, Burghfield, Berks
Printed in England by The Cromwell Press, Trowbridge, Wiltshire

British Library Cataloguing-in-Publication Data
A catalogue record for this book is available from the British Library

ISBN 0–85170–899–4 (pbk)
ISBN 0–85170–898–6 (hbk)

CONTENTS

ACKNOWLEDGMENTS

To research and put this text together, I had to talk to many people and check many details. I would like to thank Pavle Levi, Howard Feinstein, Dan Georgakas and Prof. Annette Insdorf in New York, Prof. Andrew Horton in Norman, Oklahoma, Aleksander Hemon and Milos Stehlik in Chicago, Carlos Garza and Mitko Panov in Austin, Elissa Helms in Pittsburgh, Kriss Ravetto in Los Angeles, Aida Hozić in Ithaca, Lord Puttnam, Andrew James Horton, Sophia Contento and Goran Gocić in London, Ann Miller and Piotr Kuhiwczak in Leicester, Ben Halligan in Aberystwyth, Nevena Daković in Belgrade, Zvonimir Radeljković in Sarajevo, Vesna Maslovarik and Goce Smilevski in Skopje, Aleksandar Manić in Prague, Matthieu Dhennin and Galia Valtchinova in Paris, Bojana Pejić and Igor Krstić in Berlin, Helen Loveridge in Cologne, Lorenzo Codelli and Sergio Grmek Germani in Trieste, Boris Jocić in Barcelona and Lalit Rao in Bangalore.

To enable me to complete this study, I was granted a special two-month leave from my day-to-day responsibilities at Leicester University and received financial assistance from British Screen and the British Council. For this invaluable support I am particularly grateful to Roger Dickinson, Ralph Negrine, Prof. Robert Burgess, Simon Perry and Paul Howson. I enjoyed ongoing support from the staff of the University of Leicester library, as well as at the libraries of the International Film Festival in Toronto, the BFI in London and the BiFi in Paris. My mother was here to help with the daily chores and to play with my son George when I was busy.

Last, but not least, my very special acknowledgments to Giorgio Bertellini, who opened my eyes to the virtues of traditional film criticism, to Felicity Rosslyn, who intervened just at the right time, and to Andrew Lockett, who persistently supported my writing and competently directed my cutting.

INTRODUCTION: Who is Kusturica?

On a Saturday afternoon in October 2000 I was standing in front of a small cinema near Vittorio Emanuele II concourse in Milan, in the vicinity of the cathedral square where some of the scenes in Emir Kusturica's *Time of the Gypsies* (1989) take place. I was about to enter a screening of Patrice Leconte's *La Veuve de Saint-Pierre* (*The Widow of Saint-Pierre*, 2000), starring Kusturica in the role of Neal Auguste, a nineteenth-century convicted killer. The cinema was displaying a poster of Kusturica as the dishevelled and rough protagonist, while posters featuring Juliette Binoche and Daniel Auteuil, the other members of the cast, hung in the background.

Next to me, an elegant Italian couple in their fifties passed by and stopped in front of the theatre, obviously wondering if the film was something they ought to see. They took some time to argue about the identity of the man on the poster. The woman insisted it was Gerard Depardieu, 'so rough', she said, she just loves him. The man said no, it wasn't him, 'this guy must be somebody new ... a Depardieu look-alike but definitely not him,' so who knows if he is any good. The woman went on insisting it was Depardieu, well, probably somewhat younger, but she was not so sure any more. At the end, they decided not to go for the movie and went on along the pavement to check out the other cinemas.

Reportedly, there have also been other cases of mistaken identity involving Emir Kusturica. According to one anecdote, a few years back on Kusturica's landing at Nice to attend the Cannes Film Festival, airport officials organised a formal welcoming ceremony since they thought that 'the Emir of Costa Rica' was coming. According to another one, the electoral victory of Serbian president Kostunica in 2000 was largely due to Yugoslav Gypsies, who all cast votes for Kusturica, a man who makes movies about them and therefore would be good to have as president.

So who exactly is Kusturica? In the UK and America it is probably only dedicated (and usually adoring) art-house film regulars who know his

Kusturica in *La Veuve de Saint-Pierre* (2000): 'a Depardieu look-alike',
dishevelled and rough

name. But in virtually any other country in Europe and other parts of the
world he is one of the most popular and revered contemporary cineastes.

Not only is Kusturica – with his two Palmes d'Or from Cannes and scores
of other top awards – one of the most decorated and acclaimed film directors in the world; critics have praised his extraordinary imagination and
exuberant creativity. American Michael Wilmington described him as 'a
film-maker of such prodigious and robust gifts that he makes most other
movie directors look flat-footed' (*Chicago Tribune*, 1999). And Austrian
writer Peter Handke said his films bore a Shakespearean force and were to
be admired 'for their more than merely free-floating – their free-flying
fantasy, with images and sequences so densely and evenly intertwined that
they frequently metamorphosed into Oriental ornaments' (1997, p. 7).

Others, however, have spoken of Kusturica's work as 'rambunctious' and
'over-the-top', have found his films excessively exoticised and

overdrawn and have claimed his achievements have been overrated. Some have publicly criticised his politics and have described him as an idiosyncratic opportunist.

The split in critics' ranks is also reflected among ordinary spectators. On the one hand, he has an extensive international fan following who worship his work and think of him as a film-making genius, as a person who has given them key revelations about their own existential concerns. No other director can rival his popularity across Yugoslavia and the Balkans where he enjoys a cult standing, and he is tremendously popular in Russia, Central East Europe, Italy, France, Spain and Portugal where his name is known to nearly everyone. On the other side, however, there are those (mostly from former Yugoslavia) who think of him as an opportunist and traitor, who do not want to hear his name and have stubbornly refused to even see the films he made in the 1990s.

The members of these two groups are equally aggressive and unbalanced in their reactions to Kusturica and the only thing they share is the intensity of feelings they have for the director. The strong passions around Kusturica are an acknowledgment that his films have touched audiences all over the world. But they also suggest the complexity of his personality. Indeed, Kusturica is a man who by turns comes across as charming and tactless, loyal and naïve, inspiring and ambitious, resilient and malleable, generous and petty, funny and narcissistic. And he is no stranger to controversy.

The extremities of adoration and condemnation that one comes across when researching Kusturica make it particularly difficult to stay level-headed. In writing this book, however, I wanted to be balanced and fair. So I looked for guidance and found it in two places. The first was a remark by Giorgio Bertellini, the author of one of the best critical studies on the film-maker. It is certainly not an easy thing to write about Kusturica, he admitted. But when it is done, he noted, it should be done with the intention to investigate and discuss, not to stigmatise (1996, p. 12). The second came in a comment that Kusturica made in an interview given in Sofia in 2001: 'Artists sometimes look silly when asked to talk about their life,' he said. 'One needs to judge them in the way a child judges its parents, not by what they say but by what they do when they don't know they are being watched.'

On the set of *Super 8 Stories* (2001)

So I followed these recommendations. I acknowledged the contradictions but tried to understand and make them comprehensible to others. I took into consideration what the director was saying about himself, but also looked at the reception of his films and at the various reactions to his public behaviour. I felt I needed to carry out separate investigations of his persona, his films, his artistry and his ideology.[*] What I hope to have achieved is a balanced discussion which recognises and pays tribute to his attractive and impressive aesthetics while simultaneously investigating his ideology, an aspect of Kusturica's work that has often been outweighed and obscured by the artistry over the years.

---

[*] My discussion of Kusturica's work in an industry context (production, distribution, promotion) is forthcoming.

One
The Man

Emir Kusturica was born into a Muslim family in Sarajevo, Bosnia (then Yugoslavia), on November 24, 1954.[*] He studied film at FAMU in Prague and after graduation returned to his native city to pursue a career in film-making. His first full-length feature, *Do You Remember Dolly Bell?* (1981), received the award for best debut feature at the Venice International Film Festival and his second feature, *When Father Was Away on Business* (1985), won the Palme d'Or at the Cannes International Film Festival. His last Yugoslav feature, *Time of the Gypsies*, won the Best Director award at Cannes and was released to international acclaim. By the age of thirty-five he was universally recognised as the leading Yugoslav film director.

In 1988 Kusturica left Sarajevo for New York and has since lived away from Bosnia. He refused to take sides in the conflict that broke out in his native country in the early 1990s and came to be known as a 'Yugonostalgic'. In America he made *Arizona Dream* (1993), for which he won a Silver Bear award at the Berlin International Film Festival. The film, however, was a flop in the US. Disappointed with the overt commercialism of American cinema, the director left the USA, settled in France and began to work internationally across Europe. In 1993–4 he worked on an international production, *Underground* (1995), a film which brought him a second Palme d'Or at Cannes in 1995. The film's success, however, was marred by controversy. There were allegations that it was made with the participation of the Serbian government, which at the time was perceived as the sole aggressive force behind the war in Yugoslavia. Critics in Kusturica's native Bosnia and abroad read the film as pro-Serbian propaganda and denounced the director as an intellectual traitor who had taken the side of the aggressor.

---

[*] In some interviews the director has identified 1955 as his year of birth.

His reputation tarnished by the controversy, Kusturica declared his withdrawal from film-making, a promise he broke soon thereafter by making *Black Cat, White Cat* (1998), a Gypsy-themed film made in Yugoslavia with international finance. Even though still involved in film-making (in 2001 he released a documentary, *Super 8 Stories*), for the moment Kusturica's main energies are devoted to touring as a bass guitarist of the rock group Zabranjeno Pušenje (No Smoking), with which he has played on and off since 1986. He is married and has two children, a son in his twenties and a teenage daughter.

*   *   *

Here, I will present an overview of the director's confessed allegiances – to family, friends and Yugoslavia – and will try to explain the logic of his shifting loyalties. Then I will look into his restless migrations. A veteran in dealing with the media, Kusturica has had to reinvent himself and has lived through several transformations that I will trace next. And last, I will discuss several features of his personality that seem to help in understanding the man.

Allegiances

Roots

Kusturica's family comes from Herzegovina. Back in the seventeenth century there were three brothers known by the family name of Babić, who, like all inhabitants of the region, were pressured by the Ottomans to convert to Islam. One brother remained Christian, two converted.

Is Kusturica a Bosnian Muslim or a Serb? There is much confusion around this issue, especially in the light of his dissociation from the Bosnian Muslims that came later in life. The short answer is: Kusturica is a Bosnian Muslim, but as many of the Bosnian Muslims can trace back their roots to Orthodox Serbs, the director has opted to stress the Serbian line in his origins.

Bosnia was a traditionally Christian and pagan country, the cradle of one of the main Manichean heresies of the Middle Ages. The Bosnian Muslims were formerly Christian or pagan inhabitants of the region, who were forced to convert to Islam during several campaigns after the Ottoman invasion of the land in the fifteenth century. Some of the population converted, as it was a matter of survival, but some did not. It was a time of parting when even members of the same family made different choices. The denominational split of the forefathers put brothers and cousins on different sides; their children and grandchildren would grow further apart and strands of what had once been the same family would form different communities. This historical parting along religious lines is the key event that has set out the fault lines in the region. It is reflected in the literary heritage as a tragic event that deeply divided a previously homogenous community.

The fact that the roots of his family in Bosnia can be traced back to the time before the religious parting forms the basis of Kusturica's claim that he is, in fact, of Serbian origin. In addition, his family members fought on the side of the (mostly Serbian) partisan forces during World War II, at the time when Bosnia was occupied by German Nazis and Croatian Ustasha. The director quotes this fact as yet another personal reason that makes him closer to Serbia.

Emir Kusturica is a descendant of Muslims. His paternal grandmother was a devoted follower of Islam. But even though his family were nominally Muslim, they were secular. Religion did not have much weight in the society where Kusturica grew up and denominational belonging was a formality rather than a matter of identity. School education did not include religious instruction: practising religion and learning about it was confined within the domestic sphere. Most families would observe the main holidays of their respective faiths – but these were devoid of deep spiritual significance. The differences between Muslims and Christians were made irrelevant by communism, which suppressed all religion. Since his parents were not particularly religious, the differences between Jews, Muslims and Orthodox Christians, as well as Catholic (mostly of Croatian ethnicity), played no important role in Kusturica's formation. He has indicated that he is familiar with the teachings of both Islam and Christianity, but that he feels more like a pagan (Binder, 1992).

Another manifestation of the relatively insignificant weight of religion is the fact that in Bosnia ethnic-religious communities did not live in isolation and mingled freely. Kusturica's wife is of a mixed ethnic background and it was typical for members of his generation to enter ethnically mixed marriages.

Religion became an important issue only at the time of the Bosnian War, but it did not matter before the war started and was certainly not the cause of the war. Many Bosnian intellectuals have made statements indicating that the reduction of the Bosnian tragedy to religious differences (an explanatory framework favoured by most Western journalists covering the war) is wrong and does not reflect the essence of the conflict.

No matter that many in Yugoslavia did not want to take sides along the newly created fault lines of ethnicity and religion, the break-up of the federation forced a new parting on everyone. One had to choose sides, a situation that many intellectuals described as 'madness'.

Kusturica's first choice was to stick to 'Yugoslav' identity, but it was one that had been invalidated and he was branded a 'Yugonostalgic'. He had no allegiance to the Islamic cause that seemed to inform the struggle of the Bosnian Muslims, so he publicly dissociated himself from them. He then took the extreme step of siding against what appeared to be 'his own' people by declaring that of all groups in Yugoslavia he felt closest to the Serbs, a decision that had serious repercussions on his reputation.

Family

Emir was an only child. His father, Murat, was an official in the government information bureau, a job that Kusturica likened to the one of 'Sam Lowry in *Brazil*' (Bouineau, 1993, p. 76). His father had fought on the side of the partisans during World War II and was a member of the League of the Communists. His political background positioned him beneficially – not necessarily expressed in material affluence but allowing access to certain privileges (like being able to send his son to study abroad). Even though admittedly pro-Russian, Murat never experienced the repression suffered by Soviet sympathisers as seen in *When Father Was Away on Business*. But some of his friends had perished in the camps.

Kusturica's father was a socialist-idealist, who, like the father in *Dolly Bell*, truly believed that communism would be built by the year 2000. It is not clear if he spoke to Emir of the grim sides of communism. It is possible he opted to present his son only with the utopian side of the communist ideal, like those Yugoslav parents who chose not to discuss with their children things like arrests, internment and camps. One thing is sure – that talk of communism was part of the early domestic experience of the director.

Kusturica talks of a happy childhood and of the memorable fragrance of an acacia near his window. The family lived in the Sarajevo suburb of Gorica. Like most other families, they occupied a modest flat in a communal housing project. It was a specific state socialist lifestyle that makes it difficult to locate the director's class origins on a Western scale. On the one hand, one can come across claims that his was a privileged childhood. On the other hand, he admits he mingled with some really dubious folks. In some interviews he says he is of middle-class origin; in others that the middle class did not exist. Even though these statements may seem difficult to reconcile, they are all perfectly correct. It was possible to belong to a privileged family and still mingle with street children, a situation determined by the very nature of communist housing egalitarianism.

Kusturica's parents lived in Sarajevo until the beginning of the war in 1992. Around that time, Murat got himself in trouble with the Bosnian Muslim authorities. Reportedly, he was harassed by the new powers-that-be. Emir had to intervene and arrange for his parents to move away from Sarajevo. Helped by friends, his parents settled in the Montenegrin coastal town of Herceg Novi. Soon thereafter, in October 1992, his father died of a heart attack at the age of seventy. This was a key event, adding to Emir's bitterness with Bosnia; he believed that the spirit of intolerance had effectively caused his father's premature death. On numerous occasions Kusturica has referred to the trauma of this loss and he has compared his father's death to the death of Yugoslavia.

The relationship with a father or a father figure is very important in Kusturica's cinematic universe. Critics have noted that many of the director's films contain an unresolved Oedipal situation. Judging by the frequent references to the director's own father, an investigation of this particular relationship would be of importance for those interested in approaching Kusturica's films from a psychoanalytical perspective.

Little is known of Kusturica's mother, Senka. She is rarely talked about in interviews and when mentioned it is in the context of some anecdote. I imagine her more or less like the mother-housewives in Kusturica's Sarajevo films. It is said that she woke up little Emir with the sentence: 'Good morning, Columbus!', a line used in *Arizona Dream*.

Kusturica's own family has never been discussed in interviews and he has kept an extremely low profile in regard to his personal life. He married in the late 1970s. His wife, Maja, is of mixed ethnic background (Serbian father, a survivor from the infamous Ustasha death camp at Jasenovac, and a Slovenian-Croat mother). She has been occasionally listed as a 'coordinator' in the credits of some of his films. Even though not publicly visible, Maja is known to be an extremely loyal partner and to enjoy a position of authority with her husband. She is likened to a fortress in his life. The couple's two children were born in 1979 (son Stribor) and 1987 (daughter Dunja).

Buddies

Hanging out with buddies, like Dino does in *Dolly Bell*, was an essential part of Kusturica's teenage years. They were all 'hajvani', a Turkism literally meaning 'animals' and figuratively translating as 'vagabonds' or 'bums', usually used to describe a group of mischievous male buddies loitering in small groups and having a good time. They were all fans of the Sarajevo football club Željezničar and liked playing football.

Kusturica's parents were concerned that their teenage son was mingling with the wrong crowd. One of his father's friends was a film-maker (Hajrudin Krvavac), so Emir's parents sent him to help on the set and this is how he got involved with the movies. Not that this new interest severed his links with his unworthy peers, but it made him realise that he was destined for something higher than neighbourhood fights and soccer games.

Looking back to his youth, it seems that Kusturica got the 'best of both worlds'. He granted his parents' wish to not turn into a loser by getting an education and a profession. But he also preserved a taste for the close camaraderie of neighbourhood buddies. Being a 'hajvan' supposedly means a lot

Some of the 'hajvan' buddies were cast in the early films. Mirsad Žulić (seated) was in *Do You Remember Dolly Bell?* (1981), *When Father Was Away on Business* (1985) and *Time of the Gypsies* (1989)

to Kusturica. He is particularly proud of having had such a period in his life, as it gave him the advantage of street wisdom not accessible to many.

The director persisted in his devotion to the buddy culture far beyond his adolescence. In the 1980s he readily spoke of his love of football and said he was even invited to become a professional player (Binder, 1992). Western journalists who tried to reach him on the phone after he won at Cannes complained that they could never find him at home, as he was always out kicking a ball with his pals.

In 1985, evidently not expecting to be the winner, Kusturica had left Cannes for Sarajevo shortly after the screening of his film. When asked about his absence from the award ceremony, he explained that he could not wait until the end of the festival, as he had to help a friend at home with a plumbing job. He told Downey (1985, p. 13):

> I am not the sort of director who is found in the cafés, biting my nails and
> waiting for the final decision of the Jury. So I left Cannes and went back to
> Sarajevo to help my mate fix his central heating and replace the floorboards.
> I am an expert at that!

Kusturica's involvement with the rock group No Smoking and the loosely defined movement of Sarajevo New Primitivism dates back to the mid-1980s. The New Primitives were involved in a variety of artistic activities – music, literature, theatre and fine arts – mostly within the bounds of popular culture, characterised by anti-intellectualism, mockery of their own self-confessed provincial mentality and subversive use of domestic jargon and imagery. They were best known for a series of provocative sketches on Sarajevo television that ridiculed the narrow-mindedness and incompetence of local politics. Alongside another Sarajevo New Primitive rock group, Elvis J. Kurtović and His Meteors, No Smoking enjoyed huge popularity and was a defining influence in the Yugoslav (and particularly Bosnian) youth culture of the 1980s.

Dr Nele Karajilić (pseudonym of Nenad Janković, No Smoking's front man) is one of the closest friends of Kusturica, both sharing a taste in politically incorrect humour. The very alias of Karajilić is meant to connote a combination of intellect and promiscuity, a 'Dr' who 'screws a lot' (Karajilić being evocative of two Serbian slang expressions – 'kara' for male genitalia and the verb 'karati' meaning screwing). The 'Dr' is the 'author' of an (unpublished and probably non-existent) treatise called *Provincialism as the Highest Level of Primitivism*. The New Primitives are known to call each other 'hajvani'.

Some tropes of the 'hajvan' buddy culture are used in *Arizona Dream*, where Axel, the protagonist, talks of his friend Paul's 'garbage theories' according to which the organs of a young man produce a certain amount of protein each time a beautiful woman looks at him. It is a protein 'so deadly that only a drop of it can kill a rhinoceros', a protein that runs through one's body 'like broken glass'. The actual proponent of the 'protein' mock-theories seems to be Dr. Karajilić. Kusturica, however, has embraced them and often refers to 'proteins' during his communications with audiences during the recent No Smoking concert tours.

Kusturica has clearly taken pleasure in being an ordinary pal from Sarajevo, in being part of the buddy culture that involves kicking ball or playing guitar with the local guys and hanging out on Sundays. But it is important to note that his allegiance to the buddy culture was profoundly transformed in the 1980s. He shifted from the (lower) ingenuity of neigh-bourhood buddies to the (higher) shrewdness of the New Primitives. Even though the New Primitives engaged in exactly the same activities as the neighbourhood pals, they did it as a self-conscious conceptual act. Similarly, when Kusturica told Downey he left Cannes to fix his mate's plumbing, he did not simply report a fact – he projected an image. This 'buddy' image has been an enduring element in Kusturica's public persona, being modified but still maintained as time goes on.

Sarajevo/Bosnia

Within Yugoslavia, the reputation of Sarajevo was one of a backwater, a provincial outpost with its own idiosyncratic culture. By the mid-1980s, however, the city had a thriving pop culture, with groups such as Goran Bregović's Bjelo Dugme (White Button), as well as the bands associated with New Primitivism.

Kusturica seemed perfectly happy to live and work here. He could main-tain the routine he loved – hang out with friends, make music, play football, get into brawls and be ordinary. His real commitments were to his family and friends, here and now. His growing reputation and particularly the Cannes recognition that catapulted him to fame, did not appear to make much difference. In interviews he gave after the success of *Father*, he made it clear that he intended to remain an outsider to international film circles and did not want to turn into a professional director. He preferred to continue playing bass guitar with his rock group and to go on teaching at the theatre academy in town. To an interviewer from the *New York Times* he indicated he did not identify with the type of person who would win at Cannes. 'Everything that happened went against my character, but I am learning to live with it,' he said (Kamm, 1985, p. 21). In the same interview Kusturica also said he had no plans to leave Sarajevo and was certainly not thinking of moving to Belgrade. He would consider going to live in a big European city, like Paris or London, but not to America.

And indeed, why move? Kusturica was adored in his city. A young and fantastically successful representative of what the best of the Yugoslav idea was meant to be, he was the ultimate cultural icon of the place. Known as Sarajevo's *enfant terrible*, the city had invested all its love and devotion in him.

But things were rapidly changing. It was difficult to reconcile the provincialism of the place with his new standing of a world-class film-maker. After the success of *Father*, the director's choice regarding what he would do next took on new significance. He promptly dropped a project he had committed himself to (*Strategija svrake* [*The Magpie Strategy*, 1987]). For a while, he seemed to be involved with one of his dream projects, an adaptation of Ivo Andrić's classic novel *The Bridge on the Drina*. But he soon gave that up as well, somewhat fearful of the epic proportions such a production could take. It became clear that Bosnia was too narrow for a director of his stature. From now on, all Kusturica's films were to be made outside Sarajevo. The next project, *Time of the Gypsies*, was filmed elsewhere. Shortly after completing this shoot, in 1988, Kusturica left Sarajevo for a teaching job in New York.

There was growing nationalism throughout Yugoslavia. Having left in 1988, Kusturica was not around for the intense build-up to the conflict. However, he clearly sensed something was wrong when, during a visit in 1990, he entered into confrontation with local intellectuals at an event devoted to writer Ivo Andrić. It seems this was a key episode that led to his estrangement, effectively lessening his strong links with the city.

Kusturica's last visit to Sarajevo was in 1992, around the time he worked on *Arizona Dream*. He walked down the streets with his friend Johnny Depp and realised that he had grown irretrievably detached from this place, where 'the young population was extremely defeatist and in a very aggressive mood' (Pauli, 1996, p. 135).

When fighting started in Sarajevo, Kusturica's initial reaction was to speak up for the city and to call for an international intervention. He even published a passionate piece called 'Europe, my city in flames!' in *Le Monde* on 24 April 1992, in which he wrote:

Europe, the confrontation of Bosnian Muslims and the Bosnian Serbs is not authentic, it is a fabricated one, it developed on the rubble of fallen empires that left ashes behind. It is maintained by mindless nationalist movements; it is YOUR fire, it is up to YOU to put it out.

The text suggests that it would be incorrect to argue that Kusturica had no interest or compassion for Sarajevo. He was very concerned for Bosnia, only in his own way. He would not listen to suggestions about what would be the politically correct line and he would not make the statements that others thought were right.

But soon an incident occurred that seems crucial for his change of attitude. In May 1992, Muslim militiamen raided the apartment of Kusturica's parents in Sarajevo, even taking the director's film prizes. His parents left the city shortly thereafter and a few months later his father died, away from home, in a rented flat in Montenegro.

Shortly after his father's funeral, in October 1992, Kusturica made a sharp turn in his stance to Sarajevo and Bosnia. Up until then he had voiced disapproval of the ongoing dissolution of Yugoslavia, but had not gone too far beyond expressing his nostalgia for the lost country. In an October 1992 interview for the *New York Times*, however, he made some extreme statements. Besides declaring he never wanted an independent Bosnia, he said that the new Bosnian president, Alija Izetbegović, was a Muslim fundamentalist whose government encouraged the destruction of multi-cultural Bosnia. Most importantly, however, in this interview Kusturica repeatedly stressed that in Sarajevo they wanted to kill him (Binder, 1992, p. 7).

It was around this time that Sarajevans, even those who now describe themselves as his 'former friends', rejected the director. It was a logical reaction: their darling was now claiming they were out to kill him. Since the time of these claims, many in Sarajevo have refused to see his films and do not want to hear his name.

Later on, the director claimed he was not really clear why Sarajevo had turned against him. Talking to *Cahiers du cinéma*, he explained: 'I never said anything against the Muslims; but for them it is not enough because whoever is not with them is against them' (Jousse and Grünberg, 1995, p. 70).

Besides stating that his fellow-Sarajevans would kill him, it is true that he had not bothered to say much about the Bosnians. Maybe a revealing scene about his attitude to them is the one at the opening of *Arizona Dream* where Axel (Johnny Depp) is asleep on the back of a truck in New York. It is early morning and his radio comes on. The news bulletin starts with something about 'The Bosnian Serbs ...' and then about 'The Bosnians ...' Depp wakes up and shuts the radio down. From there on the story is set in America, in the exciting free spaces of Arizona. No more Bosnians or any such annoying stuff.

Kusturica's criticism against the Bosnian Muslims is that they are equally intolerant and have contributed to the destruction of Sarajevo's multi-cultural essence to the same degree as all the others. The other reasons for his split with Sarajevo seem to be of a more personal nature. First, the director thinks that the new powers-that-be dislike his Sarajevo films, 'because I showed that Muslims could be silly, too' (Binder, 1992, p. 7). Second, he blames the death of his father on Muslim fanatics. Third, he has indicated how displeased he was to hear that his apartment, now vacant, had been confiscated by the state and given to someone else. Fourth, the Bosnians shortsightedly rejected the legacy of their great writer Ivo Andrić.

Kusturica's split with Sarajevo came into the international spotlight only at the time of the controversy around *Underground*, in mid-1995. In fact, however, it had occurred earlier and Kusturica has been *persona non grata* in Sarajevo since 1993.

The release and the international success of *Underground* in 1995 did not cause Kusturica's troubles with Bosnia, but it certainly compounded them. The Bosnian media made sure to cover his flirtations with Serbian politicians extensively. In addition, the warlord Arkan, a high-profile war criminal responsible for massacring Muslims in eastern Bosnia, attended the film's premiere in Belgrade.

Even though the film did not really deal with Bosnia, the fact it was made in close collaboration with the Serbs was the last blow that effectively severed Kusturica's links with Bosnia and fortified his ties with Serbia.

In America, one can simply turn the radio off, forget about animosities and wars and enjoy the exciting free spaces of Arizona. Johnny Depp (top) and Faye Dunaway (bottom, left) in *Arizona Dream* (1993)

Andrić

Special attention needs to be paid to the issue of Kusturica's declared devotion to Andrić, as the shift in his allegiances was played out round some highly publicised disagreements over Andrić's heritage.

Ivo Andrić (1892–1975), the Nobel Prize winner for 1961, was a Bosnian of Croatian origin (according to Kusturica, 'a Serb with a Croat name'). A titan of Yugoslav literature, his stories and novels contain profound insights into the difficult history of the region, with its complex Ottoman and Austro-Hungarian, Islamic, Orthodox and Catholic legacies. A supporter of Yugoslav unity, in his lifetime Andrić was involved in politics and diplomacy. His writing was in Serbo-Croatian, but he had used the Cyrillic alphabet favoured in Serbia. He had opposed the Croat Ustasha nationalism and had gone to the Yugoslav capital to share the fate of fellow-Belgraders, who were bombed by Nazi Germany in 1941. His two epic novels, focusing on the Bosnian experience, were written in Belgrade during World War II.

If evaluated within today's framework of strict nationalist divisions Andrić could not stand the test of 'belonging' to Bosnia. In addition, in a 1946 story called *A Letter from 1920*, Andrić had let his protagonist, a self-exiled Bosnian Jew, speak extensively of the twisted psychology of Bosnians and of Bosnia as 'a land of hatred'. No wonder his legacy was not only neglected but intentionally rejected by the new Bosnian powers; Kusturica certainly has a point when he is critical of their treatment of Andrić's heritage.

Kusturica's first adverse encounter over Andrić happened in May 1990. The director was preparing to talk at a commemorative event in Sarajevo when some people in the audience reacted adversely and they ended up embroiled in a fight.

Two years on, the disrespect to Andrić had become an acknowledged fact. The hundredth anniversary of Andrić's birth, in October 1992, went unmarked. Kusturica believed that the Izetbegović government, which had turned a blind eye to vandals' destruction of the writer's monument in Višegrad, actually favoured the desecration.

Taking up Andrić's defence as a weapon in the fight against ignorance and intolerance that was taking hold back home became a *cause célébre* for

Kusturica. In his 1992 interview with Binder for the *New York Times* he discusses Andrić at length. It is here that his old interest in filming the writer's best-known novel, *The Bridge on the Drina*, comes up again:

> Since Mr Andrić's death in 1975, Mr Kusturica has wanted to make a film based on the novel, which chronicles Bosnian history using the Turkish bridge of stone at Višegrad and the role it plays in the lives of people living along the river. 'I should make this film,' he said. 'But they would kill me.'

This statement to the *New York Times* is one of the instances of Kusturica's problematic politics. In this particular case, he may have succeeded in convincing a handful of interested parties in the West that the Bosnians, with their disrespect to Andrić (and to himself), are Muslim fanatics. But this statement had a stronger side-effect, namely to discredit Kusturica in the eyes of people back home. Earlier, the director himself had spoken of plans to make *The Bridge on the Drina* in 1986 and he had given a clear indication he had dropped the project because of logistical problems with the production (press kit for *Time of the Gypsies*, *Positif* interview, 1989). Clearly, the film did not materialise for other reasons and not because his fellow-Sarajevans were out to kill him. (At the time the project was dropped, things were profoundly different as far as Kusturica's standing in Sarajevo was concerned.) No wonder they were deeply offended.

Andrić again was at the core of Kusturica's turn towards the Serbs. The writer had moved to Belgrade during World War II, manifesting allegiance to the victimised Serbs. It seems that Kusturica, with his shift to the Serbs in times of conflict, identified with Andrić to some degree. The director has often pointed at the respect that Andrić enjoys in Serbia as an example of the superiority of Serbia over Bosnia.

Yugoslavia/Serbia

In 1993 Kusturica was still clearly identified as a Bosnian Muslim. But he was a Yugoslav first of all and did not hide how much he suffered over the country's break-up. He was a 'Yugonostalgic' and there was nothing shameful in this position. He wanted to defend the union, even though the battle was already lost.

In January 1993, he explained his position to *Le Monde*:

> I can identify with every tear that is shed over there, with every child who has
> died there, with the pain that every single person feels. But I cannot identify
> with any of the factions who are tearing each other apart or with any of the
> political concepts that they are trying to impose. Everyone has their own axe to
> grind; everyone rewrites their own version of history, with their own heroes. In
> all conscience, I do not believe that any republic, be it independent or not, is
> worth the death of a single man, woman or child. And, for my part, I have to tell
> you that whatever happens, I could never identify with any of the eventual
> winners of this horrific war.

Heymann and Frodon, 1993, p. 15

Like other Yugoslav intellectuals, Kusturica had tried to resist the perni-
cious ordinance of taking sides. Parting along ethnic divides was unnatural;
it was forced on them rather than coming as a spontaneous choice. 'I was
raised in Yugoslavia, I used to cry when listening to the national anthem and
now I have to become a Bosnian. How is it possible to defend the idea of a
multi-ethnic Bosnia?' he said (*Libération*, 27–8 May, 1995, quoted in
Garbarz, p. 16).

But he was to learn a bitter lesson: not taking sides only worked in the
tolerant West. One could be a 'Yugoslav' only away from the Balkans. Back
there one was either a Bosniak (Bosnian Muslim) or a Serb.

Faced with this difficult obligation to take sides, Kusturica did not manage to sustain his original position and did not remain a 'Yugoslav' for long.
He sided with the Serbs. In 1994 he worked on *Underground* in Belgrade and
later on, in 1995 and 1996, acted as co-director of the Belgrade Film
Festival.

Initially, it had not been so much a choice 'for' something, but rather a
choice 'against' – he wanted to show his disapproval of the nationalist madness that had taken hold in Bosnia. Effectively, however, it was also an
assertive choice, a move that engaged him with a cause, one that appeared
internationally compromised at the time.

It remains an open question why, after acknowledging faults on all sides,
Kusturica gave his unreserved loyalty to the Serbs. Why did he equate his

romantic ideal of Yugoslavia with Serbia in particular? He tried to explain it: 'I was against the selective humanism. I cannot stand the ethnic cleansing [carried out] by the Bosnian Serbs, but neither can I stand the ethnic cleansing [carried out] by the Croats' (Pflaum, 1995, p. 16). Had he cared for his popularity, he insisted, he could have waved the flag of the new Bosnia. By speaking up for the Serbs, he believed he was countering the clichés prevalent in international media. Rather than compromise his truthfulness, Kusturica chose to dispose with political correctness. The Serbs were the only ones who, at least officially, stood for Yugoslav unity and this is what he stood for as well.

What Kusturica was truly devoted to were not the Serbs but his nostalgic longing for the playful and bold spirit of Yugoslavia. In order to preserve his 'romantic dream' (1993, p. 29), he committed himself to an intimate and highly personalised vision of Serbia that was supposed to function as a sub-stitute for the tolerant, vivid and multi-cultural Yugoslavia. In choosing sides, however, he turned a blind eye to the fact that nationalist forces there used his commitment to Serbia. His shift of allegiances was problematic not because he denounced Bosnian nationalism, but because he ended up asso-ciating with another nationalism while refusing to recognise it as such.

Kusturica claimed he personally had little to do with these choices. He made sure to stress that it was not he who was rejecting the Bosnians, it was they who hated him (1992 interview, *New York Times*). It was not he who was embracing the Serbs either, they wanted him: 'I do not belong to the Serbs, but they consider me as one, ' he said (Ciment, 1993, p. 25).

By 1995, the director no longer had friends in Sarajevo. He had friends in Belgrade instead. Older ones, who had allegedly been harassed by the Muslims in Sarajevo and had found refuge in Belgrade, like the No Smoking singer Dr Nele Karajilić (Kusturica cast him in the role of a Gypsy musician in *Underground*). And new ones, most notably Milorad Vučelić, at the time director of the state-run Radio-Television Serbia (RTS), as well as the man behind Komuna, which was to become Kusturica's Yugoslav co-production company. More importantly, however, Vučelić was one of the most influen-tial people in the country, a high-profile parliamentarian and official in Milošević's socialist party. A political survivor, Vučelić was also close to

Milo Djukanović, the Western-oriented businessman and president of Montenegro, who enjoys a good reputation in international media and is also Kusturica's personal friend.

Even though Kusturica said he had 'always known that Milošević was a fascist' (Kusturica, *Le Monde*, 1995, p. 13), he had not objected to meeting the Yugoslav president via Vučelić. The meeting must have led to some mutual influencing of each other's tastes, as around the mid-1990s all three of them came to be known for their passion for cigars. Later Kusturica also claimed that *Underground* had been 'the strongest attack there has been on Milošević' (Gibbons, 1999) even though the film was co-financed by Milošević-controlled RTS and had not really come across as an attack on the Yugoslav president.

Yet another link to Serbia is via Kusturica's son, Stribor. Upon reaching legal age, Stribor had chosen to leave the West and return to Yugoslavia. In Belgrade he found a musical mentor in the percussionist Ćeda and became a drummer with the newly revived No Smoking band. Kusturica was said to have organised the first international tour of the band mostly to get his son out of Belgrade when NATO bombed the city in 1999.

By the end of the 1990s, Kusturica's 'metamorphosis' from a Bosnian Muslim into a Serb was more or less complete. Today, Western media regularly cover him as a (Bosnian) Serb. In 2000 *Variety International Yearbook* even listed him as one of the 'patriarchs of Serbian cinema' (p. 262).

Underground

Underground brought a second Palme d'Or for the director at the Cannes Film Festival in 1995. The film, however, came under critical fire from people who saw problems with the historical and political propositions upon which the story was built.[*] According to critics, the film revealed poorly concealed anti-Slovene and anti-Croatian sentiments and was thus either conscious pro-Serbian propaganda (Finkielkraut, 1995) or an uncritical glorification of the Serbs (Cerović, 1995). At the time, the Serbs were seen

---

[*] The controversy is explored in my book *Cinema of Flames: Balkan Film, Culture and the Media*, London: BFI, 2001, pp. 111–36.

as the aggressors while the newly independent Slovenia and Croatia were largely perceived as courageous fighters for emancipation from union that was forced on them and was now hindering their progress. Effectively, Kusturica was being accused of having sold out to the Milošević regime.

The controversy created a significant noise, but the debate remained cryptic for larger audiences. Those who defended the film, like Austrian writer Peter Handke (1997), put forward purely artistic criteria and insisted that aesthetic value rendered politics unimportant. Those who attacked it, like Alain Finkielkraut and Stanko Cerović, referred to political correctness and insisted it was important that the film be judged by political criteria. By choosing to make a film in Belgrade at the time when Serbia was at war with his own native land, others insisted, a Sarajevan director like Kusturica was committing a specific act of treason.

It is important to stress that *Underground* was not a film about the tragedy in the director's native Bosnia (as mistakenly perceived by many critics) but about the past fifty years in Yugoslavia's history at large. Many of those knowledgeable in Yugoslav affairs, the director included, saw the Bosnian conflict as a by-product of the conflict between Slovenia and Croatia on the one hand and Serbia on the other. The real issue at stake, therefore, was whether the film had been backed by the Serbs as part of their ideological war against the newly independent westernmost republics of Yugoslavia. There were allegations of strong financial support for the project by Serbia's oppressive regime. The alleged financing was doubly problematic, as it appeared to have taken place in violation of the international economic embargo against Serbia that was in place at the time. The producers' reaction to the scrutiny was to become secretive and to evade direct discussion of *Underground*'s finance and in particular of Serbia's participation.

The initial plan had been to make *Underground* at the Barrandov studios in Prague, with artistic contributions from people from all Yugoslav nationalities but excluding financial contributions and any other form of official Yugoslav participation. Kusturica himself, however, welcomed Serbian involvement, mainly for creative reasons. He was particularly unhappy with the light in Prague that was so different from Belgrade and suppressed his inspiration. He much preferred that the film be shot in its original setting:

'Prague was chosen as the best alternative to Belgrade, which is a pity. But now, things have changed and we will be able to continue the film in Belgrade,' he said (Ostria, 1994, p. 80).

Underground was a highly personal take on Yugoslav history. It followed an extended script that presented a complex and elaborate overview of historical responsibilities for Yugoslavia's break up. The film's long version, shown in 1995 on Serbian television, had addressed the causes of the conflict and attributed concrete guilt and responsibilities. The derivative theatrical version, shown at Cannes, had stressed moral and existential problems and significantly tamed the attribution of historical guilt.

At the time of the film's international release, Kusturica did not insist on blowing the trumpet about the film's specific take on Yugoslavia's failure. He had his chance to offer his concrete views to a genuinely responsive audience in Serbia (in fact the only mass audience to whom his vision really mattered). When promoting the film in the West, Kusturica more or less gave up on discussing the role of various nationalities in the break-up. Instead, he resorted to explaining the film within the vague terminology of an 'earthquake' and a 'slippery region', where ancient historical struggles come to the surface in violent cycles. He effectively hid from the Western public his views on the origins of the crisis (they were not likely to be understood in the West anyhow). Instead, he sold a less politicised image constructed around the dominant Western perceptions of the Balkans as an exotic and wild place.

Nonetheless, challenged by critics, he had to defend himself against allegations that Serbia was trying to use the film as a propaganda tool. The film reflected his views on Yugoslavia's break-up and, indeed, he believed that the Slovenes and the Croats had betrayed the Yugoslav idea while the Serbs had bravely stood for it. But the prevalent international public opinion in 1995 differed.

In his defence, Kusturica could choose between two options. One was to enter an open confrontation with his critics, fight for his opinions and openly admit the financial and moral backing the Serbian government had given to the film. But the odds were against him and there was no realistic chance his views would be understood or appreciated. The damage that such a scenario would inflict on his career could be devastating. The other line of defence was to stay afloat and create a rhetorical smokescreen that would divert attention from the main issues raised by the critics. He would not need to change allegiances and neither would he need to fight for them in public. Kusturica chose to go for this second option and did it in three ways:

- by spinning the ideological message of the film by moving the focus from the issues of concrete historical guilt into the blurred realm of ancient Balkan hatreds (in a range of press conferences and interviews given in 1995).
- by ridiculing his critics (*Le Monde*, 26 October 1995).
- and finally, by publicly announcing his retirement from film-making in December 1995.

None of these really worked and the best remedy proved to be the oblivion that came in time. The director's reputation was damaged, but not too badly. He soon managed to reinvent himself and came up with a new public persona, seemingly turning his back on convoluted politics and striking a pose of intense artistic exuberance.

In the course of the controversy Kusturica's loyalties were put to a more serious test than he had ever expected. The stakes were his allegiance to 'Yugoslavia' on the one hand and his career on the other. The outcome was one that lacked closure and catharsis: both career and allegiances were saved, a survival secured in compromise.

*   *   *

Shifting loyalties is an ongoing process for Kusturica. Today, he often travels to Montenegro, a place to which the director developed a romantic attachment in the 1990s, as if to compensate for his ruined links with other parts of Yugoslavia. Having recently become a French citizen, he was described by a British journalist as a 'part Montenegran [sic] and part Serb', in possession of French and 'Montenegran' passports (Tobias Gray, *Financial Times*, 29 July 2000).*

---

* I should note that at the time of writing in 2001, Montenegro is part of rump Yugoslavia and not issuing passports on its own.

Over the past few years Kusturica has repeatedly indicated that he has started work on a memoir with the working title *Diary of a Political Idiot*, which will contain autobiographical accounts of twelve select episodes of his life and will be published in France. But the project has dragged on and so far he has not been able to complete it. The title, however, suggests that this book will cast new light over the director's passions and allegiances.

Movements

Yugoslavia was the only state socialist country that permitted its citizens to travel abroad freely. In comparison to people in the Soviet bloc, who were kept in isolation, Yugoslavs enjoyed a privileged position as they could get exposure to the West. I am not aware if Kusturica took advantage of this freedom to travel in his teenage years. By the age of forty-seven, however, he had lived outside his native country for extended periods of time, adding up to eighteen years.

Since 1988 he was mostly based in the West. It has been a period of restless moving. As if anticipating this lifestyle, in 1990 the director said 'I'm like a Gypsy myself. I like changes, I see myself moving all around for the next 10 years' (Thomas, 1990, p. 6).

By now Kusturica is a firmly established diasporic director. In the foreseeable future, he will most likely remain based somewhere in the West while maintaining a nomadic lifestyle. It is important to note, however, that his movements have not expanded or changed the scope of his concerns. His genuine allegiances still rest with his family, his friends and with Yugoslavia. The only dimension that life in the West seems to have added is the self-promotion savvy he has acquired in the course of it all.

Prague

Kusturica studied film in Prague, at the famous FAMU School, between 1973 and 1977. At high school he had been a bad and unruly student. His acceptance to film school had to be arranged in order to 'tame' him. 'The Czech culture helped me to somewhat soften my character and enabled me to look with irony at my stubborn views of life,' he said (*Standard*, 17 March 2001, http://www.standartnews.com/archive/2001/03/17/art/index.htm). At first he stayed with an aunt, whose partner worked for the Yugoslav news agency Tanjug in Prague at the time; later Emir was able to share a room at the student dorm Hradebni.

FAMU had a great reputation in Yugoslavia. Aleksandar Petrović, a veteran of Yugoslav cinema, was its graduate. A few years before Kusturica's arrival several other Yugoslavs had graduated from here (Serbs Goran Marković, Srdjan Karanović and Goran Paskaljević, Croats Lordan Zafranović and Rajko Grlić). By the time of Kusturica's arrival, they had all launched promising careers back home where they came to be known as the Prague group. Other graduates included Slovenian cameraman Vilko Filač and Croat editor Andrija Zafranović (brother of director Lordan), both of whom were to become close collaborators later on.

At FAMU, Kusturica was in the class of director Otakar Vávra, a veteran of Czech cinema, reputed to be a consummate survivor. The times were grim, particularly for the intelligentsia. It was in the aftermath of the 1968 Warsaw pact invasion that followed the Czechoslovak attempt to establish 'socialism with a human face'. Many of the reputed film directors, whose works made up the Czech New Wave, were either banned from filming and had their works shelved (Věra Chytilová, Jiří Menzel), or had emigrated (Ján Kádár, Vojtěch Jasný, Miloš Forman, Ivan Passer, Ján Němec, Evald Schorm and FAMU's leader, screenwriter František Daniel).

Nonetheless, the students were exposed to the works of these masters and films such as Forman's *Konkurs (Competition, 1963), Cerný Petr (Black Peter, 1963), Lásky jedné plavovlásky (Loves of a Blonde, 1965), Horí, má panenko (Firemen's Ball, 1967)* and Menzel's *Ostre sledované vlaky (Closely Watched Trains, 1966)*, were well known and discussed in class. The students also had exposure to a range of cinematic works from various other film traditions – the best of Soviet cinema, Italian neo-realism, French New Wave, as well as classic examples of American *film noir* and slapstick comedies. Kusturica was particularly impressed by Scorsese's *Taxi Driver* (1976), Coppola's *Godfather II* (1974) and Hitchcock's *North by Northwest* (1959).

Students were being trained to work in all capacities in the film-making process. They made shorts, which were then presented at student competitions. It was at one of these, at Karlovy Vary, that the director got his first award, for the diploma short *Guernica* (1977).

Emir, however, did not like Prague. The city's imposing architecture and its monuments remained foreign to him. Weekends in Prague were particularly depressing – when taking strolls on Sunday, amidst the great baroque buildings, he felt intimidated and dreamt of returning to Sarajevo, 'scared by this great cultural tradition that I did not have in my native country. I felt like a fish flying over deserted streets' (Ciment, 1993, p. 21).

America

The 1985 success of *Father* was a crucial point in Kusturica's career. The degree of his creative freedom had expanded enormously. He now had the backing of powerful Western production and distribution mechanisms. He no longer depended on the approval of the local authorities for the projects that he wished to film. He had the chance to work on projects that he wanted, to go abroad or stay. He was still very young, in his early thirties. Bosnia was already too small for him. So he opted to go abroad.

In 1988, after the completion of *Gypsies* but before its release, Kusturica left Sarajevo for New York. He took up the visiting teaching appointment at Columbia University that Miloš Forman, chair of the film studies programme, offered him. According to Kusturica the intention was to have him 'succeed' Forman there (Heymann and Frodon, 1993, p. 15).

In Sarajevo he had taught an actors' class at the local theatre academy. At Columbia he simply continued his teaching routines, only in a new environment and with new, American students. The New York engagement was temporary and the director was thinking of returning. But things back home were changing. Appalled by the growing nationalism in Yugoslavia, he grew increasingly estranged from the developments there. He occupied a flat in Manhattan's Morningside Heights and his family were to join him there.

But Kusturica never came to think of America as home. On the contrary, he felt like 'a fish out of water' (Bouineau, 1993, p. 56). On many occasions he made fun of American kitsch and on many others he spoke of the adverse role that the American media played in covering the Yugoslav conflict.

He said he felt like a 'fish out of water' in America, yet Kusturica looks at his best in these photos from the set of *Arizona Dream* (1993)

Still, he committed himself to making a film in America, one that was supposed to express his vision of the American Dream. The shooting period of *Arizona* coincided with the rapid aggravation of the Yugoslav conflict, the war in Croatia and the beginning of the Bosnian War. Talking to a French interviewer, the director recalled: 'I remember the terrible regret I was experiencing every single day during shooting, for having stayed there, in America, for not having returned home, to Sarajevo. This feeling of being cut into two. Every day I was telling myself I will leave and every day, no, I stay' (Heymann and Frodon, 1993, p. 15).

His choice to stay and work played a crucial role in his ultimate alienation from Sarajevo. But it also led to his estrangement from America. The completion of the film was followed by a period of serious disagreements with the US producers. Unable to settle the disputes and unwilling to adjust to the commercial attitudes of American film-making, Kusturica moved back to Europe and has taken every opportunity to express his anti-Hollywood feelings.

Europe/France

Of all European countries, Kusturica seems to like Italy the most. It may be because Italy is so popular with most Yugoslavs, dedicated followers of Italian fashion and lifestyle. References to Italian popular culture abound in Kusturica, from Celentano's song in *Dolly Bell* to the *Alan Ford* comic in *Black Cat*. The director has indicated that if he had the same working conditions as he does in France, he would rather live in Italy.

But Kusturica has lived in France since 1993–4 and since the late 1990s has been a French citizen, which gives him particular advantages in accessing European and French funding for film.

In addition, he has often complimented the French for understanding real cinema and thinks of France as 'the country that has most respect for auteurs' (Bouineau, p. 71). He may not identify very deeply with the tradition and the culture of France, but he is conscious of his need to be liked and in this respect France is certainly the place to be. True, there are some problems with those French intellectuals who attacked him over *Underground* and his Yugo-politics. But the director has chosen to ignore them, by dismissing people like Alain Finkielkraut as biased Croatian cronies and by calling Bernard-Henri Lévy a 'vulture'.

As things stand in 2001, Kusturica's main residency is in a Normandy village about two hours from Paris. He also has a small apartment in the artistic Marais district of Paris, an apartment in Belgrade, property in Montenegro, as well as a yacht that is reportedly kept on the Greek island of Corfu, opposite Albania. He is also said to be making arrangements for the return of his Sarajevo apartment.

The boat is the place he thinks of as 'home', he told journalists in 1999. His preference for such a volatile moving concept of home may be taken as an indication of his acceptance of a fluctuating, diasporic identity.

Diasporic Yugoslav

> The Sarajevo of which you talk no longer exists in Sarajevo: it is present in
> Bologna, in Belgrade, in Stockholm, everywhere in the world, even in Japan.
>
> Kusturica, quoted in Boni, 1999, p. 22

Today, Kusturica is more than ever conscious that the diasporic condition is not a temporary one but has gradually become a durable mode of existence. By his own choice, he leads a restless semi-nomadic lifestyle in the context of which 'home' is only an element and by far not the most important one. He maintains several residences but does not spend much time in any given place, most of the time he is either on the road or in various sites, engaged in transnational projects that involve a variety of locations and a motley international entourage.

Over the past decade, the Western media have covered the issue of Kusturica's emigration in a variety of ways. Reputable newspapers have called him a 'refugee' (*International Herald Tribune*) or have claimed that he 'fled' Bosnia (*Financial Times*). Kusturica, however, left Bosnia before trouble started in Yugoslavia. His leaving was not in response to the events there, but was a reaction to the new possibilities that had opened up for him and that he took up. By leaving Bosnia in 1988, he did not emigrate and even less did he become a refugee. He simply joined the class of cosmopolitan commuters to which most prominent film-makers belong. Meanwhile, a number of things happened that made him change his mind about return. Kusturica chose to stay in voluntary exile in the West.

In a way, his case is similar to Miloš Forman's, who had left Prague mostly because, after winning awards and attracting international attention, he had received interesting offers from Western-based producers. The beginning of his career abroad coincided with the political showdown in Prague, which he undoubtedly disapproved of. Similarly with Kusturica, he left Yugoslavia to take up the possibility to work abroad and not because of political disagreement. Events that coincided with this step certainly contributed to his decision not to return, but they were not the factor behind his leaving. While mainstream film criticism in the West persistently presented Forman as a typical post-1968 exile from Czechoslovakia, the director has made sure not to engage in any overt statements identifying politics as the main reason for his migration to the West.

Kusturica is probably most accurate when he describes himself as a *Gastarbeiter* (*travailleur étranger*) (1993, p. 35). He has rejected the attitude of painful displacement and overwhelming uprootedness characteristic of exilic directors. Instead, he has managed to turn his life abroad into an endless source of excitement, enjoyment and inspiration. He has the energy and the stamina to be a diasporic Yugoslav – because, as it has become clear by now, one can be a 'Yugoslav' only in diaspora.

A particularity of Kusturica's diasporic existence is his close involvement with the Belgrade-based branch of his former group No Smoking. The group claims to be comprised of musicians who have not taken sides in the Yugoslav break-up, but it notably includes only those former members who moved to Serbia. (Yet another No Smoking band is based in Sarajevo and includes those members who stayed in Bosnia.) For the period 1999–2001 the director performed as No Smoking bass guitarist for the group's two European tours, known as 'Collateral Damage' and 'Unza Unza Time'. He has vested his name in the group's promotion. If it were not for this marketing device I doubt whether the band would have received a fraction of the media attention that it has been granted. Praise of the band's eclectic Balkan Gypsy-techno rock style was the subject of Kusturica's latest film, the *Super 8 Stories* (2001), a documentary in which he attests his allegiance to the 'buddy culture'.

Kusturica's close commitment to No Smoking supplies a closure to the volatile experiences of the past decade. By securing the international success of the band, he satisfies an inherent deficiency in his own diasporic exis-tence. He can continue living abroad, which means a significant degree of freedom and relief of the awkward politics of what used to be Yugoslavia. As of recently, due to his considerable artistic leverage, he has been able to 'import' his buddies and the idiosyncratic humour and jokes that he appreci-ates so much. He now seems to have finally established a new 'home away from home', having secured not only the territory but also the entourage and having recreated the 'hajvan' culture that he must have missed throughout.

Reinventing oneself

To the handful of Western journalists who met Kusturica in the early stages of his career he appeared shy, childlike and unspoiled. Today, after more than a decade in the West, he has given hundreds of interviews and press confer-ences. In his dealings with the media he acts with an ever-growing public image savvy and lately comes across as a 'gruff' and 'pugnacious' veteran.

The metamorphosis in Kusturica's media persona, from an unpreten-tious provincial chap into a weary rock-star, can be traced in media clippings:

1985: Mr Kusturica is genuinely uncomfortable, even before a public of one, from his tousled brown curls to his unmatched denim jacket and jeans down to his scuffed, rubber-soled shoes. His reticence stems from palpable timidity rather than public relations artifice.

New York Times

1997: A big bearded man with greasy hair, tight jeans, a dirty black denim jacket and a scar under one eye, he looks more like a 70s rocker than a director who won the Palme d'Or twice by the age of 40. Clearly wary of the press, he has an understandably hunted air.

Sight and Sound

1999: He is tanned, fit, with glint in his eye and a jaw that speaks of determination.

International Herald Tribune

1999: A great bearded bear with a half-chewed cigar sticking out of his mouth like a Balkan Castro. You can see him carrying a Kalashnikov as easily as a camera until you look into his eyes. They are the largest, softest, brown eyes I've ever seen on a man.

The Guardian

2001: Dressed in a beret, chewing on a cheroot, thrashing away on his bass, Kusturica did indeed look like a Balkan Lee Van Cleef.

Time Out

Looking beyond the media image, I will outline several of the director's most important transformations.

At the time of *Black Cat, White Cat* (1998)

Talented Yugoslav film-maker

In the context of Yugoslav cinema Kusturica is in a category by himself. But this is how things look now, twenty years into a successful career. At the time of his beginnings, it seemed natural that he had a defined place among other Yugoslav film-makers. It appeared logical that he was listed in the ranks of the so-called Prague group, comprising directors who, like him, had been educated at FAMU: Marković, Karanović, Grlić, Zafranović and Paskaljević. Like them, Kusturica claimed artistic roots in Italian Neo-realism and French poetic realism. His first film had raised concerns very similar to theirs. Statements that Kusturica made at the time suggested that he would like to be seen as part of this new direction in Yugoslav cinema. But even though he could be (and sometimes has been) formally listed as a member of the Prague group, he was never accepted and treated as one of them. Not only because he graduated a few years after the others: it seems there were members of the group who were reluctant to take him on as a younger associate. Whatever the reasons, Kusturica must have been badly hurt over this rejection. Later on, as he became better known, he articulately dissociated himself from the Prague group. His recent invectives against Goran Paskaljević, the Prague group director who is best known internationally and who also lives in France, have been well publicised. In interviews, Kusturica has called him 'jerk' and 'asshole' and has claimed that Paskaljević has been accusing him of collaborating with Milošević just to get attention for himself (Gibbons, 1999, p. 3).

As far as Bosnian cinema is concerned, Kusturica never seems to have worked closely with the other two best-known directors from Sarajevo, Bahrudin (Bato) Cengić and Ademir Kenović. *Dolly Bell* was made locally in Sarajevo at a time when Bosnia's cinematic output averaged two or three films a year.

At the time when *Dolly Bell* won in the debut film category at Venice, Kusturica was in military service. It took the intervention of émigré director Vuk Babić to allow him to come to Venice and receive the award. It was a boost for the young director's position on the domestic film scene where he came to be known as a promising talent.

The key turn in Kusturica's career, however, came in 1985, when he, quite surprisingly, was awarded the Palme d'Or at Cannes. Even though part of the official competition, the director had not expected to receive an award and had not even stayed until the end of the festival.

The Cannes recognition substantially changed his career. Had he not received the top award, he would have continued as a talented Yugoslav film-maker. After Cannes, however, he had become an artist of international stature. Within his native Bosnia he was catapulted to fame, with the Cannes award having nearly the same effect as the Nobel Prize for literature for his compatriot Ivo Andrić in 1961. It was the second major international recognition for the culture of this small landlocked republic.

Kusturica was now facing an important choice: to remain a talented Yugoslav director, or to try becoming a film-maker of international calibre. He opted for the high profile international career.

After a period of hesitation about several other projects, Kusturica made *Time of the Gypsies*, a film that marked a clearly articulated change in his artistic style. The film was released as a Yugoslav production, but was in fact made with international financing and marked the beginning of Kusturica's career as an international film-maker.

Recognised international film-maker

Kusturica also remains in a category of his own in the context of international cinema. He does not belong to a group or a movement and he is not known to be particular friends with any other film-maker of similar standing. The only exception appears to be Miloš Forman, who was instrumental in launching his international career. But there is not much evidence of a cordial relationship extending beyond the late 1980s.

Encounters with producers – people like Harry Saltzman, David Puttnam, Claudie Ossard, Pierre Spengler and Jean-François Fonlupt – have been more crucial for Kusturica than encounters with other film-makers. It seems, however, that the group of directors working with the German company Pandora and producer/distributor Karl Baumgartner – Jane Campion, Aki Kaurismäki, Chen Kaige, the Quai brothers and Tajik Bakhtiar Khoudoinazarov – form a loose group of 'auteurs', among whom Kusturica is a key figure. Actor Johnny Depp is the only Western film personality of whom the director has spoken as a personal friend.

He prefers to work with a permanent and supportive creative team. 'The people I work with become involved very early,' he said in *Underground*'s press kit. In the movie-making process the director sees himself as the nucleus of a small universe around whom the other team members gravitate in concentric circles. It is the harmonious functioning of such a structure that allows a film to materialise successfully.

Even when working on productions abroad (like *Arizona Dream* or *Underground*), Kusturica has surrounded himself with Yugoslavs who have been his closest collaborators on shooting, editing and musical score. There may be a number of reasons for this loyalty to a Yugoslav team. The main one, I believe, is the ability of the director to converse with these key people in his native language. He may have considerable fluency in English, but he is much more articulate in what used to be called Serbo-Croatian and this certainly makes a big difference to successful communication on subtle creative matters. So does a shared cultural background with these crew-members.

If one scrutinises the evolution of Kusturica's team, however, one cannot help noticing that the past few years have been a period of transition characterised by the gradual desertion of earlier team members and the attempts of the director to build up a new circle of co-workers. For the last decade Kusturica has officially broken up with some of the collaborators who contributed greatly to the reputation of his films – examples include screenwriter Abdulah Sidran and composer Goran Bregović. Other key collaborators – such as cameraman Vilko Filač or editor Andrija Zafranović – are also notably absent from the credits of Kusturica's latest films.

The second Palme d'Or at Cannes, which the director received for *Underground*, made him one of the few who have received this top cinematic award twice. Only two other cineastes – Francis Ford Coppola (*The Conversation*, 1974 and *Apocalypse Now*, 1979) and Bille August (*Pelle the Conqueror*, 1987 and *The Best Intentions*, 1992) – have enjoyed the same level of recognition at Cannes. Even though the controversy around *Underground* was not great publicity, he managed to keep on top by turning the tables on his opponents and treating them as narrow-minded sectarians.

The director is well aware of the importance of reputation and knows that the big A-festivals make (and destroy) reputations. He has worked hard to win festival recognition for all his films and remains more concerned for the reception of his films on the festival circuit than ticket sales. Besides Cannes, Venice and Berlin, his films have won awards at many other international festivals, from Saõ Paulo to Moscow. Even though he has not had an Academy Award, some of his films have been entered by Yugoslavia for the Oscars and have been nominated for the Golden Globe and for the European awards.

Twenty years into his international career, Kusturica has received a number of other awards as well: the prestigious Rossellini award for directing in 1989 and the Fellini prize awarded by the director's native city of Rimini, in 1996. He has served as a president or as a jury member at many bigger or smaller international festivals. His work has been the subject of numerous panoramas and special events. This type of publicity and promotion appears more important to him than the commercial performance of his films, as box office success cannot really measure the type of achievement Kusturica cares about.

Ideally, Kusturica would like to be left working without thinking of costs. He is more concerned about getting inspiration and sustaining it than about the financial part. But even so, he knows how to approach and play the system of international film financing and how to take advantage of production mechanisms across Europe. He has considerable practical savvy in issues of exposure and does not miss promotional opportunities, maintaining a high profile presence in the media, at festivals and a variety of other venues.

The director has said that today he can finance a movie on his name alone and can easily find $5–6 million for a film. In addition, there are a number of high-profile actors who are prepared to work with him, whose names could pull in further financing (Kaufman, 1999). But he has also said he is prepared to work with a digital camera and a small budget, a statement confirmed by his latest film, *Super 8 Stories*, an internationally financed inexpensive documentary.

It has been of particular importance for Kusturica to preserve the position of an independent auteur working outside the mainstream but nonetheless popular with wide audiences. He is an outspoken opponent of the Hollywood system and has repeatedly said that European art cinema should mobilise itself and provide an alternative. Such statements are part of what has established the director as a darling of the art-house film press. Magazines such as *Positif*, *Cahiers du cinéma*, *24 Images* and *Sight and Sound* have diligently covered all his undertakings since *Time of the Gypsies*.

By now, he has learned how to live with fame and is frequently in the spotlight of international media. In the mid-1990s some critics suggested that Kusturica was laying 'a claim to the throne of European cinema, vacant since the death of Tarkovsky' (Mars-Jones, 1996, p. 7). It is still to be seen if this is, indeed, the case. At the moment it appears he is moving in a different direction by playing the role of the versatile artist.

Universal artist

In the press kit for *Gypsies* Kusturica indicated that he has a particularly difficult time with 'the reason for making a film' as he simply does not believe that one 'should make movies according to some industrial model'. It is his heart that leads him every time he ventures into filming, not his head, he said. To him, filming means transforming his energy into light. He admits that during shooting he is occasionally overcome by lack of confidence and by the feeling it is all coming apart and that he simply cannot stand the financial worries. And even though he always seems to find the psychological strength to complete the film, he has spoken of the process of filming as a long and painful suicide. Upon the completion of each film, he is so exhausted that he thinks of buying a farm and spending the rest of his life working the fields.

Having said numerous times that he does not want to institutionalise himself in cinema, lately Kusturica has come closer than ever to becoming a universal man of arts. One of his new pursuits is acting. In 2000 he starred opposite Juliette Binoche in Patrice Leconte's *The Widow of Saint-Pierre*; his performance was unanimously described as competent. He looks, indeed, as if created for the role of Neal, a simpleton who has killed and has been sentenced to death but has to await execution at the remote island of Saint-Pierre. Kusturica has since agreed to be cast in Neil Jordan's next film.

Writing is another path explored by the director, who said that cinema was 'closer to the art of the novel, to the epic form than to theatre' (Ciment and Codelli, 1989, p. 8). In the early 1980s he published a dozen or so short

A universal artist, as seen in
Super 8 Stories (2001)

stories in the Sarajevo monthly *Svjet*, one of which, called 'Below and above, above and below', was translated into French in 1995. In 1985 he co-scripted a Bosnian film and occasionally talked of writing a play and a novel. In 1989 he again talked of the novel which, once written, he intended to turn into a film. Even though his autobiographical *Diary of a Political Idiot* is on hold for the time being, he is planning to complete it one day.

Most important to him, however, is his life as a touring bass guitarist of No Smoking. While he thinks of cinema as an all-consuming process of martyrdom he has described making music as a cathartic activity.

He hasn't explored fine art so far and is known to be not particularly skilled at drawing. But he engaged in an artistic happening at the Milan furniture fair in 1999 where he 'interpreted a room'.

(http://www.designboom.com/eng/agenda/fanclub/fankusturica.htm)

Understanding Kusturica

This man's character is so abundant and contradictory that it is nearly impossible to balance all aspects. I feel, however, that I should at least point out those features of his personality that appear most persistent.

In 1981, when he won at Venice, *Time* magazine wrote that 'the winner is nobody from nowhere', Kusturica said (Ciment, 1998, p. 19), a sentence that would remain with Kusturica for a long time. It is the ambition to expose the inherent racism of such derogatory treatment that has kept him motivated. Further motivation comes from the realisation that his success has made many people jealous. A feeling of vulnerability compounds the consciousness of people's envy; he suppresses it by working even more ambitiously, against the grain. He is aware of his provincialism but he never feels apologetic about it. Instead, he defiantly and proudly asserts his provincial origins as a source of unshakeable self-esteem and maintains a consistent preoccupation with insignificant people inhabiting unknown places. Does he care about fame? Yes, a lot. But he is a man who would resolutely put to work his obstinacy and make fame adjust to his ways, rather than change his ways for it.

To Kusturica, the state of maturity is associated with decline and squalor. In 1997 he told a *Sight and Sound* interviewer that great directors begin 'making shit' beyond the age of forty-two.

Most of his films are coming-of-age stories that display a specific reverence to patriarchy by leaving classical Oedipal confrontations open-ended and evolving around straightforward situations of betrayal and revenge within family-like settings. Kusturica's case, both biographically and cinematically, proves a fertile ground for those working in the psychoanalytical paradigm. He has referred to evasive childhood memories to explain his Yugonostalgia, which, in turn, has defined the ideology in his films. A scrutiny of his relationship with his father and his devotion to the 'hajvan' microcosm may open up paths to understanding his idiosyncratic vision of history and social conflict.

Kusturica admits to having an explosive nature. He is known to have fought not only over Andrić but also on many other occasions. Favourite anecdotes include his 1993 duel challenge to nationalist leader Vojslav Šešelj and his brawl with a Serbian right-wing politician in 1995. He was not exactly tolerant towards those who criticised him over *Underground* and reacted to critics quite aggressively by pronouncing them ignorant and biased.

Vincent Gallo, an actor who himself is known for explosive temper, said: 'Emir is a wonderful, compassionate person, but he is a bully, a comedic bully' (Feinstein, 1996, p. 78). On various occasions Kusturica has spoken of a 'manic-depressive nature', which he thinks is reflected not only in his manner of working but also in the cyclical essence of his movies. During shooting he is said to be very nervous, in the grip of powerful and extreme mood swings. When on the set, he admits, he lives through moments when he is ready to walk out, as he does not believe he can bring the project to a meaningful conclusion. But at the end he somehow survives the crisis and manages to bring things to a successful end.

'I am very impulsive and very stupid sometimes, but I am very clean,' the director said (Gibbons, *Guardian*, 1999, p. 2). Many see him not as a shrewd manipulator but as a passionate creative artist, who wants to have fun, live happily and make films in spite of everything. Thus, on each of the numerous occasions when Kusturica has come across as politically incorrect he has also come across as impulsively truthful. With a few exceptions, he has been truly persistent in his unwillingness to adjust to what may be perceived as appropriate in order to preserve what he spontaneously feels is right.

This truthfulness, particularly as it is revealed in his attitude to the West, is one of the reasons for Kusturica's huge popularity across the Balkans where many see him as a role model. He is adored for being uninhibited and audacious, for being successful without compromising, for daring to be unceremoniously arrogant and still be accepted and celebrated internationally.

Last but not least comes the director's narcissism. He needs an audience and he needs to be loved; in 1995 at Cannes he declared this need to be his only reason for making movies. He does not want to commit himself to existing causes because causes originate and end with him. In his extreme individualism, Kusturica does not differ substantially from many other big artists. He is the ultimate romantic, creating in all possible forms, withdrawing and then returning playfully, recreating both himself and the world in an ascending process of artistic renewal.

Two
The Films

As far as I am concerned, I have set myself a personal artistic programme. I began with two films, which I consider like literary classics. And then I played with a rock group before making *Time of the Gypsies*, which resembled a punk concert, with the same permanence, intensity and highly emotional aspect. For me, this was the equivalent of a Sex Pistols concert. I then made *Arizona Dream*, which I compare to a rug, an old Bosnian rug, rather than to a film. I have tended to assemble disparate elements of this rug, to weave them together. Now, what I would do with *Underground*, it is a circus. This was the only possible way to treat the continuing problems of Yugoslavia.

Kusturica, quoted in Ostria, 1994, p. 78

The work of Kusturica can be divided into several periods. The early one comprises student shorts and two television features he made for Sarajevo television in the late 1970s. The narratives and the cinematography of this period are strongly influenced by Czech cinema.

Then come 'the Sarajevo films' – *Do You Remember Dolly Bell?* and *When Father Was Away on Business* – both set in Sarajevo, both drawing on experiences of Bosnian Muslims in Tito's Yugoslavia, both subtle psychological dramas.

Time of the Gypsies marks a clear stylistic departure from the earlier works. It is here that we see the beginning of what can now be described as Kusturica's ultimate style – unleashing a Fellinesque imagination and a temperamental exuberance, achieved through combining fantasy elements, music, camera and *mise-en-scène*. Even though the subsequent films differ substantially from each other, I believe that everything Kusturica has made since 1989 – *Arizona Dream*, *Underground* and *Black Cat, White Cat* – belongs to this period of, in his words, 'grandiloquent frescoes'.

There is another possible grouping of Kusturica's films, evolving around themes. In the films he has made up to now, he keeps returning to three main topics. There are three coming-of-age films (*Dolly Bell*, *Gypsies* and *Arizona*), two films about the collisions of history and individual fate (*Father* and *Underground*) and two Gypsy-themed films (*Gypsies* and *Black Cat*).

Early films

As a teenager, before going to film school, Kusturica made two shorts, *Dio istine* (*Part of the Truth*, 1971) and *Jesen* (*Autumn*, 1972). He does not attribute much importance to them and has called them impressionistic and naïve. In 1977 he developed a synopsis for a feature called *Kuća u slijepoj ulici* (*House on a Dead End Street*), which remained unrealised. It was strongly influenced by the work of Ivica Matić, from whose script Kusturica was to make his first full-length feature later.

Kusturica's diploma film, the twenty-five-minute long *Guernica* (1977), which won an award for best student film at Karlovy Vary, is based on a novella by Antonije Isaković and set in an unnamed Central European town in 1941. The film is marked by a strong Czech influence, not only in its style but also in its choice of the Holocaust topic. This is the story of a Jewish teenager whose family is asked to undergo a medical examination for Semitic racial features. The father tells the son that their long noses will be checked. The apprehensive boy gathers family photographs, cuts out all noses from the pictures and assembles a collage resembling Picasso's *Guernica*. The key role that collage and montage play in the film is an early indication of the director's later interest in a range of post-modernist forms of expression. The long nose is an item in Kusturica's image inventory that reappears later on. It is a Cyrano de Bergerac nose accessory that Marko plays with in the extended version of *Underground*. An actor playing Cyrano, who receives a parcel containing a real cut-off nose, will be the protagonist of the planned film *The Nose*.

Nevjeste dolaze (*The Brides Are Coming*, 1978)

Kusturica's first full-length feature, made for Sarajevo television in 1978, was *Nevjeste dolaze*. It is based on a script by Ivica Matić, who had intended to film it himself but had died prematurely at the age of twenty-eight.

The film, set in present-day Bosnia, treated controversial taboo topics like sexuality and incest and reportedly was never broadcast. 'The Brides Are Coming undoubtedly remains the most courageous plot that I have ever treated,' Kusturica said. 'It talks about the transmission of energy within a family' (Bouineau, 1993, p. 76).

The protagonists are Jelena, a strong-willed matriarch, who runs an isolated mountain inn with her two grown-up sons – Martin and Jakov (Bogdan Diklić). Previously a thriving spot, no customers come to the inn any more; the place is deserted as if cursed. Martin has been married to Kata for five years, but she has failed to conceive, so Martin regularly mistreats her, a 'barren cow', and beats her savagely at night. Jelena, the mother, seems to approve of this treatment, while Jakov, the younger brother, who is in love with Kata, is suffering silently. Kata refuses to run away with him and all he can do is to listen to her midnight cries while, in a scene suggesting incest, lying in his mother's embrace.

One night, Jakov, who can no longer endure listening to the abuse, runs away from home. In the morning Kata is dead. Jelena and Martin bury her. Soon thereafter, however, they find the grave desecrated and empty. A young girl appears out of the blue. Even though Jelena opposes her presence, she soon becomes Martin's new 'bride'.

An ageing lumberjack, Nikola, also comes uninvited and it soon transpires that he is Martin's father who has left the region years ago. Nikola has come to die, as he says, and even though Jelena initially rejects him, they soon make up and retreat to her bedroom.

The inn is made over and crowds of customers miraculously arrive. Martin is excited by the good turnout. When the customers start calling for the new girl to sing, she is reluctant. But as Martin insists that she does, she stands up and delivers a plain performance of the popular Italian song Parla mi d'amore, Mariu, and soon all in the pub join in with the singing. Agitated and drunk, the men assault the 'bride'. Martin cannot do much to prevent the violence, while the returnee father caresses his unsuspecting mother upstairs.

The next morning, Martin lies dead in the pub, probably stabbed. A truck dumps the 'bride' in the forest, near Kata's grave. She wanders between the trees and soon finds Jakov, whom she joins. It is as if Kata has been resurrected, to take revenge and become a new bride to a new groom.

*   *   *

Brides makes distant reference to a number of Greek tragedies, the stories of Eteocles and Polyneices (rivalry between brothers), Sisyphus (Kata is asked to carry buckets full of water to the top of a hill where Martin kicks them back down), Oedipus/Jocasta (incestuous relationship) and Ulysses (Nikola's return). More importantly, however, the film marks the beginning in Kusturica's interest in matriarchy, a motif that will appear again in his later work. We also hear Jakov talk of poetry and of experiencing oneself like a fish, a motive that will come about in *Arizona Dream* and of 'above' and 'below' (*gore–dole*), one of the basic dialectical oppositions in Kusturica's aesthetics.

This is probably the only film of the director where the assault of a woman takes such a key place in the narrative. Had *Brides* been as widely known as Kusturica's other films, the proponents of the 'primordial' interpretation of the Bosnian conflict in the 1990s would have quoted the film as a premonition of the mass rapes to come.

Brides is influenced by Czech cinema, inhabited by typical New Wave personages like land surveyors, insurance agents and delivery drivers (Kusturica in a cameo appearance). Stylistically, it is indebted to Tarkovsky, with the most interesting shots of the film literally re-staging set-ups from his *Solaris* (1972) and *Zerkalo* (*Mirror*, 1975). For example: an extended shot taken from the interior of a house that tracks action taking place outside through a series of windows; or a long shot slowly gliding over a stretched out set-up of objects that include a fish in a bowl, a shoe and empty bottles; or a revolving shot that keeps bumping at the same person in a room; and yet another revolving shot, taken from within a circle and tracking the circular movement of the protagonist who is trying to break into the circle. Some of the visual motives in the film are recycled in Kusturica's later work – a man on top of a ladder being shaken in *Arizona Dream*, a colourful parasol and a whirligig in *Black Cat* and the red flowers found in most of his films.

Bife Titanik (*Bar Titanic*, 1979)

TV Sarajevo again produced Kusturica's second television film in 1979, *Bife Titanik*. Based on a story by Bosnian novelist Ivo Andrić, it was co-scripted by Czech screenwriter Ján Beran and is one of the rare cases when the Sephardic Holocaust has been treated in cinema.

The story, set in the 1930s and early 40s, evolves around two protagonists – the photographer Stjepan (Bogdan Diklić), a Sarajevan Croat, and the pub-keeper Mento Papo – Herzika (Boro Stjepanović), a Sarajevan Jew who runs the 'Titanic Bar'. This is the only one of Kusturica's films in which parts of the story are told in a voice-over, as if narrated by Andrić himself. It is also the only film that tells the story in retrospect, opening at its culmination point and then going back to trace how the confrontation between the protagonists came about.

The Jew is a short and insignificant man of limited intelligence and interests, barely concerned with anything beyond drinking and gambling. He spends his days and nights in the semi-darkness of the pub he runs, often joking that he is a transatlantic captain. His lover is the Croat Agata, a dominatrix-type blonde, who makes a living sleeping around.

Unlike Mento, whom we only see in his adult life, Stjepan's story is traced back to his teenage years. We are made witnesses of some formative adverse experiences at home and his place of apprenticeship. After years of travels, Stjepan returns to Sarajevo where he establishes a photographic studio. He is tall, blond and good looking, but also a secluded loner who plays out his insecurities by dressing up and pretending he is someone else, never able to commit to a single identity.

When Nazis and Ustasha occupy Sarajevo, Stjepan joins the Ustasha police. Mento Papo, the Jew, is quickly ostracised. No one comes to his pub any more and his vulnerability grows by the day. He is the black sheep of the tightly knit Jewish community, so when he turns up for help, the rabbi points out in agitated Ladino that Mento himself has chosen not to be a proper Jew and therefore cannot expect much support. He hides in the darkness of his deserted bar, waiting for the fate to strike.

One night Stjepan comes to Mento's 'Titanic' in his Ustasha uniform. They have never met face to face before. Stjepan starts blackmailing the Jew

for money. Mento attempts to get himself off and negotiate: he does not
have the money, but he will 'supply'. It is not money, however, that Stjepan
is after. It is the pleasure of dominance, not the imaginary gold that he is
asking for. Excited by the power of his uniform, Stjepan fires shots at the
pub-keeper. Images of the passing transatlantic liner flash in Mento's mind
while he lies dying in the corner of the bar, under the picture of the Titanic.

*   *   *

Since *Titanic*, which won a prize at the television festival in Portorož (now
Slovenia), Kusturica has not had the chance to return to the Holocaust topic,
nor to Ivo Andrić's literary universe. This film, however, marks the beginning of some of the thematic preoccupations that will remain with the director later on: the relationship between individual and history, the interest in
identity and manipulation. Approaching the subject matter in a way typical of
Central European cinema, the historical confrontations are reduced to interpersonal relationships between concrete and equally contemptible people
who end up on opposite sides, respectively as victims and perpetrators. The
victimised protagonist is a chicken-hearted individual who feebly allows
himself to be sacrificed. The troubled perpetrator is an insecure individual
who joins the Ustasha police to become empowered, a character very close to
the peasant protagonist of Louis Malle's *Lacombe Lucien* (1974). They inhabit
the multi-ethnic universe of interwar Bosnia, but their ethnic identities are
clear-cut – the victim is a Sephardic Jew rejected by his community, the perpetrator a Bosnian Croat endowed with the power to kill by the Ustasha
regime. The theme of the film is not solely the Holocaust but also the betrayal
of the Croats within the Yugoslav federation during World War II, an issue
that will continue concerning Kusturica for many years ahead.

Long tracking shots, a preference to brownish darker colours and interiors and a fairly slow pacing give this film the specific feel of a direct
predecessor of *Underground*. Scenes shot in a mirror, as well as mirror
images multiplied in duplicate and triplicate, as often seen in the director's
later films, make their first appearance in *Titanic*. The source of light is
often included in the frame, usually a cone-shaped lamp that hangs from
the ceiling and casts big shadows on the walls. The disturbing swinging

light, after a bullet hits the lamp under the low ceiling of the pub, dramat-
ically enhances the violent confrontation of Stjepan and Mento.

Bar Titanic looks and feels like a Central European film, both in terms of
story and style. The weak protagonist is very much like Tono from the Slovak
Holocaust classic Obchod na korze (The Shop on Main Street, Ján Kádár and
Elmar Klos, 1965). The scenes of women looking out of windows to empty
streets are reminiscent of Ján Němec's Czech Holocaust classic Démanti noci
(Diamonds of the Night, 1963), and many pub scenes, of Zoltán Fábri's
Hungarian classic Az ötödik pecsét (The Fifth Seal, 1976).

The Sarajevo films

The film production of Bosnia at the time Kusturica made his early features
was small in size. Only a handful of people worked in film-making. Most of
them depended on financing from television and the production and post-
production of all feature films was realised with the involvement of the
other republics.

Bosnia had a reputation as a deeply provincial place. Today Sarajevo may
be seen as a focal point of multi-cultural cosmopolitanism. Back then, however, it was simply a parochial backwater where 'sad, drunken railway men
and taxi drivers'[*] (Kusturica, 2001) of various ethnicities mixed together in
pubs. It was this provincialism and the traditionalism of the patriarchal and
yet cozy isolation of Bosnia that Kusturica's early films reflected. These
films confirmed his reputation as an indigenous director whose truthful
and self-confessed devotion to his roots highlighted the way in which he
first came to be known.

Sjećaš li se Dolly Bell? (Do You Remember Dolly Bell?, 1981)

Sjećaš li se Dolly Bell? is based on an autobiographical novel about screenwriter Abdulah Sidran's childhood in the early 1960s. Kusturica also collaborated on the script and is said to have insisted on livening it up by bringing
in some comical elements. The local company Sutjeska Film produced it
with the participation of TV Sarajevo. The film won awards for best script

---

[*] Kusturica in conversation with Elena Dragostinova in Kultura (Sofia), 23 March 2001, p.8.

and best young director at the Yugoslav national film festival in Pula (now Croatia) in 1981, and was offered an entry to the Venice festival at the end of August where it won the award for best debut feature.

The coming of age of the sixteen-year-old protagonist Dino (played by the twenty-year-old Slavko Štimac) during that summer vacation is marked by three events – he has sex for the first time, his father dies and he becomes a guitarist and singer of the first local rock band. By the end of the film Dino grows out of the domesticity that, with the shared bedroom and the Sunday lunch visits to relatives, takes up a substantial part of his life at the beginning.

Dino lives in a two-room house with a leaking roof in a hilly neighbourhood overlooking Sarajevo. He is the middle one of three brothers, between Kerim and Midho and they have a little sister. His father, Mustafa (Slobodan Aligrudić), is a restaurant manager and a diligent communist. His mother, Sena, is an unremarkable housewife, mostly concerned with household chores. The family has been on a waiting list for state accommodation for more than six years and no change is in sight. Dino hangs out with the pals from the neighbourhood, goes to the local youth club and keeps a rabbit in

Like Kusturica, Dino lives in a hilly neighbourhood overlooking Sarajevo

the adjacent pigeonhouse. He is interested in personal growth, spirituality and hypnosis (elements that Kusturica claimed to having brought into the script) and studies the method of nineteenth-century French psychologist Emile Coue, continuously repeating the incantation: 'Every day in every way, I am getting a little better …'

At a screening of Italian Alessandro Blasetti's *Europa di notte* (*Europe by Night*, 1959), a documentary on nightlife, Dino first comes across the erotic ideal of 'Dolly Bell', a Western striptease star. Like his teenage pals, he is preoccupied with the secrets of sexuality. In the evenings they spend outdoors in the dim light of an electric bulb, they tell each other stories of sexual adventures but they are all acne-scarred virgins.

A nice-looking unobtrusive lad, Dino may be the first one of them to get laid. Pog, a local thug recently out of jail (played by Kusturica's buddy Mirsad Žulić) appears with a young woman and asks Dino to hide her for a few days in the pigeonhouse. Introducing herself as 'Dolly Bell', she is from a nearby village and, as it becomes clear, will become a prostitute working for Pog.

Over the several days Dolly Bell spends at Dino's they grow attracted and nearly engage in what would be his sexual initiation. The idyll is abruptly ended, however, as Pog comes to collect the girl. He has summoned several of the local boys to induce her into the trade. Dino's loyalties are split as he watches his neighbourhood buddies rape Dolly Bell, powerless to intervene. He then helplessly watches her taken away on Pog's motorbike.

Later that summer he hears that Dolly Bell may still be around and discovers her performing a striptease at a local hotel. They finally have sex and Dino fights Pog in an open confrontation.

Dino's father, Mustafa, has discovered Dolly Bell's presence and is intrigued and excited, discreetly taking pride in seeing his boy as a womaniser. The father's curiosity about the sexual affairs of the son balances well his otherwise satirised image, a caricature of a devout communist. He is a Muslim, but not being overly religious he drinks alcohol and occasionally a lot. Then he comes home late and, in high spirits, assembles the male members of the family around the table and holds deliberations with minutes and resolutions for the record, like real Communist Party meetings. He mostly speaks in quotes, supposedly by Marx but in fact agitprop platitudes

– 'communism will arrive by the year 2000', for example – picked up during ideology education sessions. Dino, who is in favour with his father and is preferred over the other siblings, attempts to argue occasionally, but the paternal authority is too strong to be resisted effectively. Nonetheless, father and son remain entangled in a continuous dispute that plays out around the inherent contradictions of communist ideology in favouring the social over the individual. Mustafa, the communist, believes in the objective socio-economic forces that drive human fates. Dino, the hypnotist, believes in the subjective psychological energies that shape human individuality. Kusturica has said that many of these dialogues are based on the type of exchanges he had with his own father (Ciment, 1995, p. 24).

Mustafa also argues with Dino's uncle (Pavle Vujišić) while visiting his place for a weekend lunch, again over politics and ideology – matters in which neither one of them has any real say, but which nonetheless dominate every conversation. But there is an existential side to his father as well: he is occasionally sad, growing older and experiencing a mid-life crisis. During the visit to the uncle's a sudden downpour forces everyone to run from the yard into the house, but the father chooses to remain outside, in the rain, alone and vulnerable.

Soon thereafter Mustafa is diagnosed with cancer and after a sojourn in the local hospital is released to die at home. The death of his father, which happens in Dino's presence, is a serious blow to the family. They have just received the long-awaited relocation order and are preparing to move. Mustafa, who dreamt of communism, is leaving them right at the time when they seem to be a step closer to the perfect social state. He symbolised patriarchy against which Dino would have rebelled in due time. But with his death patriarchy is prematurely terminated and thus saved as a sweet memory and source of painful nostalgia.

All these personal events are interlocking parts in the wider context of Dino's socialisation. The comrades of the youth department are concerned with juvenile delinquency, so as a counter-measure they put together a rock band of local boys. They pick Dino as lead guitarist and vocalist, a role he definitely enjoys but which comes to him effortlessly, assigned from above, thus making him and the band part of the system. Their favoured song is

Adriano Celentano's *24 mila baci* (*24,000 Kisses*), but Dino also adapts a local melody, a 'sevdalinka', to a rock rhythm thus modernising and westernising the heritage. The image of a high-rise construction site at sunset that repeatedly flashes in his mind makes an essential part of his dreams of modernity. It is a dream of another life, not present here and now, but conceivable and achievable, one that will come along with the personal perfection, as we all get better 'every day in every way'. At the end of the film, the family will be seen moving to the new place, which could also be the high-rise of Dino's dream.

*   *   *

To Bertellini, *Dolly Bell* is influenced by Fellini, particularly in the way memory is used as introspection into the collective popular history (1996, p. 39). It would also be possible to interpret it in the veins of the Italian neorealist tradition, attested by the use of numerous references to Italian popular culture. But the influence of Czech and Russian film-making is equally strong, if not even more pervasive. Many of the narrative details in *Dolly Bell* bear the charm of Menzel's and Forman's tongue-in-cheek stories set in an identical social environment in the early 1960s. No longer as literal, Tarkovsky's influence is clearly sensed in all scenes involving water, rain and windows.

Today, many Yugoslavs speak of *Dolly Bell* as Kurturica's best film. They love it because it is very humane and likeable without being intrusive and because it takes them back to a long-lost period of childlike serenity. In addition, *Dolly Bell* remains a little-seen film and there is a touch of the esoteric about it. While below the artistic achievements of Kusturica's later film-making, it is a film that emerges from the director's symbiosis with his native community, a durable and deep bond that promises to be everlasting.

Dolly Bell creates a distinct image of Sarajevo and its people. The city, combining rural and urban dimensions, is shown as an idyllic place irretrievably changed by modernity. High-rises and neon signs gradually take over the cobblestone lanes of Turkish-style houses in stone and timber. Set amongst Bosnian Muslims, a community of which very little was known until the troubles of the 1990s, it shows them as people preserving patriarchal domesticity while displaying a secular attitude to Islam. Dino belongs to a generation that, in his father's views, will not only build communism but also live in it. Locally, it will be a special brand of communism, with a streak of endearing traditionalist nostalgia.

Otac na službenom putu
(When Father Was Away on Business, 1985)

Scripted by Abdulah Sidran, again partially based on a 1972 memoir of the writer and again set among Sarajevo Muslims, *Otac na službenom putu*, a 'historical love film', goes deeper in exploring the complex relationship of individual and history. While in *Dolly Bell* the narrative barely went beyond the immediate family and neighbourhood, here more powerful political forces shaped the plot line. The multi-cultural nature of Sarajevo is also clearly seen – there are Muslims (the family), Orthodox Serbs (Joža's family), Croats (the neighbours Franjo and Ankica, Zijo's wife), a Hungarian (the neighbour Ilonka) and Russians (the doctor's family in Zvornik).

The director, who co-wrote the script, was not even born at the time when the events were taking place; thus the film does not reflect personal experiences. But Kusturica insisted that the story be told from the child's point of view (and not from the mother's, as Sidran had originally conceived it). He also used to sleepwalk as a child, an autobiographical element of fantasy quality he brought to the script.

It took about two years to secure approval and finance for the project, perhaps because of the subject matter, which was politically awkward but also suffered from overkill at the time (Downey, 1985). The film was supposed to be produced by Sutjeska Film, but they were procrastinating, possibly hesitant about the potential political implications. After a false start in 1983, another local company that traditionally only made shorts, Forum Film, was persuaded to take the risk and back the project. Sarajevo television was also involved. In an interview for the *New York Times* Kusturica set the budget of *Father* at around $200,000.

The film opens in Sarajevo in June 1950 and runs through to July 1952. Malik (Moreno Debartoli), who was born in 1944, is the little son in an

Mirza, Meša and Malik: a family portrait of the early 1950s

urban family of Bosnian Muslims. He lives in a house in Sarajevo with his
mother Sena (Mirjana Karanović) and father Meša (Miki Manojlović), older
brother Mirza (Davor Dujmović) and their maternal grandfather (Pavle
Vujišić). The extended family also comprises Malik's two maternal uncles,
one, Zijo (Mustafa Nadarević), is a secret service policeman who lives on his
own and the other one, Fahro, is a sailor in the military who visits home only
occasionally. The only relative on the father's side is an uncle who is a bar-
ber, suggesting that Meša may be one of the frequent cases where a man of
peasant origins would marry up in the city and remain reliant on his wife's
dwelling resources.

Meša is a good-looking vivacious *bon vivant*. Apart from being a philanderer, he is shown to head a happy family, with the exception of the somewhat
tense relationship with the father-in-law. He spends time with his boys and
is closely involved in Malik's upbringing: he teaches him how to keep his feet

parallel when walking, like a real communist, because 'communists have an inborn aesthetic sense.' But Meša suppresses his communist beliefs when it comes to paying respect to the old Muslim traditions and arranges for the boys to be circumcised.

The snapshot of the family is taken shortly after the 1949 split between Stalin and Tito, a period that distinctly marked all aspects of life within Yugoslavia. It was a period in which it was particularly important that everybody affiliated with the party (to have a career at the time one needed to be a party member) and demonstrated loyalty to the cause of Yugoslavism and independence from the Soviets.

It is precisely loyalty that comes under scrutiny in Meša's case. A cartoon in *Politika* depicts Marx sitting on a desk and Stalin's portrait hanging above him on the wall, hinting at the Soviet cult of Stalinism and the alleged neglect of the legacy of authentic Marxism. 'They have gone too far,' Meša comments in disapproval of the cartoon. Unfortunately, this comment is made in the presence of Meša's mistress, Ankica (Mira Furlan), who is angry about his procrastinating about divorce. Soon afterwards she takes an opportunity to report Meša to the authorities, represented in this case by Zijo, Meša's secret service brother-in-law, who sees the same cartoon as 'witty'. Meša is arrested and sent to a labour camp, the coalmine of Lipnica, where he ages and sobers up about life. Ankica marries Zijo.

Left to cope on her own, Sena can barely make ends meet; she pays some visits to Zijo and to Ankica and the reasons for Meša's imprisonment gradually emerge. While the father is 'away on business', the boys behave as model children, dressed up in formal grey raincoats and suits. Unlike the older Mirza, Malik does not seem to understand what exactly is happening and interprets the events in his own way. In response to his father's absence, he begins sleepwalking. The sleepwalking incidents usually occur in reaction to some adverse experience, but he quickly learns how to use his somnambulism to manipulate the adults. While visiting the father in the camp Malik does not let his parents have sex, demanding instead that undivided attention is given to his sleepwalking.

The father is released in about a year and all the family is interned in the eastern Bosnian community of Zvornik, on the Drina River. Things seem to get better, even though Meša carries on with his womanising. He even takes Malik along on one of his 'whoremongering' trips, during which yet another sleepwalking incident occurs. While the father is busy with a woman, Malik wanders into the forest and is found at dawn by the alarmed party members on the edge of a cliff.

During the Zvornik period Malik falls in love for the first time – with the astonishingly balanced and mature Masha, daughter of the local doctor, a descendant of White Guard Russian émigrés. While sleepwalking one night, Malik wanders into her bed and in the morning they are allowed to take a bath together. In a subtle scene of sexual awakening, Malik is seen intensely staring at Masha's genitals through the bathtub water while evidently ashamed of his own private parts. But Masha suffers from leukaemia. An ambulance takes her away one night and she never returns.

By the summer, the family is back in Sarajevo. The final part of the film takes place on 22 July, 1952, the historical date of Yugoslavia's national team's football match against the Soviets. It is also the wedding day of Sena's younger brother, so all the family members have gathered in the courtyard to celebrate. Even though a time for celebration, the wedding is also a time for settling scores. Meša insists that Sena, now in advanced pregnancy, make up with her secret service brother. Even though she resists it, she finally obeys and reluctantly sits down on the table next to him. In his drunk remorse, Zijo violently hits his forehead against the table and bleeds.

Zijo's wife, Ankica, ends up in the basement of the house, lured by Meša and they have sex. Meša is quite violent, he wants to punish her. Malik, who has finally got his leather football and is playing in the yard, observes the scene through the window. It is a moment of illumination – the boy comes into possession of a first-hand knowledge of sexuality, as well as of his father's infidelity. A few moments later, when Meša reappears in the yard, Malik has matured and looks at his father in a new, critical way. Ankica remains in the cellar and tries to commit suicide by hanging herself on the toilet, but fails.

The family is together again, united by the heated radio-voices of the broadcast of the football match between the Soviet Union and Yugoslavia. The Yugoslav team beats the Russians 3–1 and qualifies for the Olympic quarter-finals, the joy of the victory symbolically asserting the triumph of the political line over which they have all suffered and are now redeemed.

But the family is not really together any more. Too many things have happened; the knowledge of all the betrayals and infidelities is too heavy a burden. The film ends with a wedding, the beginning of something new, but also with the departure of the grandfather, who decides to leave the house and withdraw in disapproval. The bittersweet void of his departure reasserts nostalgia for the traditional ways that, in their opposition to the corrupt and compromising world of the new, preserve whatever moral purity is left.

*   *   *

In *Father*, Kusturica's style is economical, relying on close pans of the protagonists and on psychological details. The Czech influence is still clearly visible – in the way the private links up with the social, in the close-ups, in the subtle humour. At the same time, the setting of some scenes, such as the landmark wedding sequence, which will claim a key presence in Kusturica's films from now on, is in many ways reminiscent of Fellini's *Amarcord* (1974). Some of Kusturica's trademark tropes, like the failed hanging attempt, appear here for the first time. Some other tropes that play a prominent role here, like the extreme close-up of a fan to suggest psychological tension, are among the devices that the director will abandon. There is increased attention to the colour composition of every scene, with a white spot that is frequently balanced by a red spot within a frame.

Even though the story seems to be told from the point of view of six-year-old Malik, the child's own interpretative framework dominates the narrative only in select instances (Horton, 1988). In most other cases Malik's commentaries on the behaviour of adults are clearly adjusted to allow the viewer to easily overcome the child's perceptive angle and decipher what actually takes place. Horton classified the narrative as a latent Oedipal confrontation that never comes to realisation, as no destruction of the father ever comes about. Like *Dolly Bell*, *Father* asserts rather than subverts paternalism.

Quite unexpectedly, *Father* won the Palme d'Or, the top award at the Cannes Film Festival. The prize came as a shock to the festival's audience.

In *Cahiers du cinéma* (373, p. 6), Serge Toubiana described the reaction at the announcement of the award:

> When Forman, the jury President, dropped the bomb in the Grand Auditorium – in front of TV cameras as well – the hall's reaction was delayed for a quarter of a second. And for a reason: only a few among the 2,800 present had had the curiosity to go and see the film eight days earlier. Hence the slight silence that preceded the polite applause. One prefers not to ask oneself what would have been the reaction of this audience had they seen this film.

The Cannes festival has a good record of appreciation for Eastern European cinema. The career of Czech Miloš Forman, who presided over the jury in 1985, was also launched here in the 1960s. Many critics believed that the Palme d'Or would not have gone to *Father* had it not been for this émigré director's endorsement of the Czech cinematic sensibility so clearly felt in Kusturica's film.

It is difficult to say today if *Father*'s somewhat lukewarm reception in the West was a reaction to the film itself or to the award it had been granted. Many critics thought the film was overrated. They treated it as yet another endearing family story so frequently seen in East European and Italian cinema. *Cahiers du cinéma* claimed that the film was insufficiently cinematic, following the script too closely and not making much use of the specific means of film language. Kusturica was still a long way from becoming a Cannes darling. *Father* may have won the Palme d'Or, but the international response remained reserved for another four years, until his next film, which finally broke the ice.

The film-maker at large

The Cannes award for *Father* and the years that followed brought about two distinct developments. First, Kusturica was soon to break into the world at large, which eventually led to a painful split with his own roots as he could not possibly be as loyal to Sarajevo as before. Second, he finally arrived at what can be described as his specific cinematic style, which only came into being with *Time of the Gypsies* and which he has since been perfecting, with various degrees of success, in *Arizona Dream*, *Underground* and *Black Cat, White Cat*.

Dom za vešanje (Time of the Gypsies, 1989)

For me, this film is an important stage in my work: it truly reveals my concept
of cinema.

Kusturica, quoted in Beauchamp and Grugeau, 1990, p. 58

For *Dom za vešanje* Kusturica collaborated with a new screenwriter, Gordan
Mihić. The idea for the film came from Kusturica, who had been impressed
by an article about the illegal trafficking of Gypsy children over the Italian
border, one of the top media stories in Yugoslavia at the time. But the story
was too trivial as it were, so Kusturica and Mihić began working together to
enrich the main plotline. Thus came the stories of growing up, betrayal, love
and death that were appended to the original idea. In a Skopje prison
Kusturica had the chance to talk extensively with a young Gypsy, stories of
whose life in Italy he also used. Rajko Djurić, a well-known specialist on the
Roma, acted as a consultant.

Kusturica's interest in the topic is not unique in the Balkan context as
the Gypsy theme has been prominent in the cinema of Yugoslavia. Many
elements of earlier Romani films were recycled in *Time of the Gypsies*. The
geese wandered in from Aleksandar Petrović's *Skupljaci perja* (*I Even Met
Happy Gypsies*, 1967), the Roma celebrating St George's Day in the water –
from Stole Popov's documentary *Dae* (1979), the accordion-playing Romani
– from Slobodan Šijan's *Ko to tamo peva* (*Who is Singing Out There*, 1980) and
the little Romani beggars in the Western metropolis – from Goran
Paskaljević's *Andejo Čuvar* (*Guardian Angel*, 1986).

Gypsies involved production companies from Belgrade, Forum Film-
Sarajevo, international finance and had a British-based producer, Harry
Saltzman of Smart Egg Pictures. Officially it was a Yugoslav film but was made
with the support of Columbia Pictures' David Puttnam, who, even though
Columbia was not listed as an official co-producer, put in a reported $1.2
million and guaranteed the American distribution of the film. This signifi-
cantly higher budget, a lavish one for the Yugoslav conditions, allowed
Kusturica a great luxury: he could work without being pressured by schedules.

The pre-production period took nearly eight months and the shooting
nine months, from 14 September 1987 to 4 June 1988. A variety of locations

With Ljubica Adžović

were used. The set for the Gypsy ghetto was built in the vicinity of Šutka, a Romani neighbourhood near the Macedonian capital of Skopje. The dream sequence of lovemaking in the water was shot on the rivers Treska and Vardar, near the Skopje suburb of Saraj. Other scenes were shot in Slovenia, Milan and Rome. Later on, a television mini-series was put together in Yugoslavia; it used the same material but was made without Kusturica's creative participation.

Two assistants travelled around the country and took photographs of Roma. A select few were interviewed. Kusturica looked for amateur actors whose energy was displayed on their faces, an approach that paid off with the discovery of Ljubica Adžović, who played the grandmother.

*   *   *

The film opens like Fellini's *Amarcord* – with a local fool directly addressing the audience. We are taken into the Romani ghetto where Perhan (Davor Dujmović), a Romani teenager with telekinetic abilities, lives in a makeshift shack with his charm-healer grandmother Hatidža (Adžović), his crippled

Perhan's main possessions are a pet turkey and an accordion

little sister Danira and his compulsive-gambler uncle. The family survives on a tiny income from a limestone oven they maintain. Perhan and Danira's mother has died prematurely and their father, who was a soldier from Slovenia, has never been around. Hatidža gives Perhan a pet turkey, which he carries everywhere and likes to hypnotise.

Perhan is in love with Azra (Sinolička Trpkova), a fair-skinned Romani teenager. They want to marry. But Azra's mother does not want to hear about it as she thinks her daughter deserves a well-to-do husband. In a dream sequence Perhan is seen flying over hills with his turkey. The Gypsies celebrate St George's Day (*Ederlezi*) in a beautiful river ceremony involving water and fire. Azra and Perhan make love in a boat, a sequence located between dream and reality.

The events are precipitated by the arrival of Ahmed (Bora Todorović), a crime lord nicknamed 'the Sheikh', who lives in Italy with his brothers. Perhan's uncle suffers losses while gambling with Ahmed's brothers and, in desperation, tries to get the money he owes from his mother, but she cannot bail him out. The uncle is so enraged that he lifts the makeshift house with a crane and leaves it hanging in the air, in pouring rain (hence the title of the film, *A House for Hanging* in literal translation). Having effectively left Hatidža, Perhan and Danira without a roof, by the next morning the uncle has also turned Perhan's pet turkey into soup.

The Sheikh agrees to take Perhan's little sister, Danira, to be treated in a hospital in Slovenia. Perhan decides to accompany his sister and they leave with the Sheikh soon thereafter. The grandmother stays behind, not even knowing if she will ever see them again. On the way, the children are visited by their mother's ghost.

In Slovenia, the sister is admitted to the hospital, or so Perhan thinks. He wants to stay with her, but it is impossible to arrange, so he succumbs to Ahmed's insistence that he comes to Italy. They arrive at a trailer campsite near a highway overpass in the outskirts of Milan. At first Perhan is not involved with the routines of the gang and simply observes the daily activities of Ahmed and his brothers who run a ring of children – beggars, pickpockets and prostitutes. But soon he is coerced to join in. He reluctantly learns the art of burglary and begins making good money, some of which he manages to hide away. But he is

The only means Hatidža can use to provide treatment for her ill granddaughter is the network of fellow-Romani

lonely and sees painful dreams that cross-reference Milan's cathedral with an idealised image of his distant home. In the course of six months he becomes the Sheikh's favourite; when Ahmed is betrayed by his brothers and suffers a stroke, Perhan takes over the ruined business. He is sent back to Yugoslavia to bring new child-beggars and re-establish the operation.

Back home, Perhan soon realises that the Sheikh was lying when he claimed to be building a house for him. The worst, however, is that he finds Azra pregnant – he is tipped off that it is probably from his uncle. It is a disaster, he is alone, betrayed and destroyed and has to start piecing his life together again. Azra insists that the baby is his and was conceived on St George's Day, but he does not believe it. He agrees to marry her, but plans to give away the unwanted child as soon as it is born. After the wedding they leave to go back to Italy, gathering children to take to Italy on the way. Azra keeps swearing that Perhan is the father, yet he is adamant about giving the baby away.

As soon as they arrive at the campsite in Italy, Azra, who is still in a wedding gown, escapes in desperation. She goes into labour by the nearby railway tracks, her body levitating against the background of a passing train and a haunting musical score, the veils of her white gown floating around and giving this magical image a sublime, harrowing quality. Almost immediately after the birth she dies in Perhan's arms. Ahmed's wife takes the baby boy into her care.

Soon thereafter, the police raid the campsite, Ahmed is arrested and Perhan escapes. Eventually, he learns that the Sheikh also lied about his sister, who was taken out of the hospital the day after she arrived to an unknown fate. Perhan grows determined to seek revenge.

Four years later Perhan accidentally stumbles on his sister on the streets of Rome. He has been working as a criminal on his own and has made a good fortune. He now learns that Danira was forced to be a beggar for Ahmed's clan and they are also raising his little son. Ahmed has made up with his brothers and is marrying a new wife later that same day.

Danira takes Perhan to the Gypsy camp amidst Roman ruins in the outskirts of the city and they abduct his son. Perhan sends Danira and the boy back to Yugoslavia by train and promises to follow them soon. But before that, he has to settle accounts with Ahmed. He returns to the camp where the wedding is in full swing. He pretends to beg Ahmed for forgiveness and is invited to join in the celebration. Seated at the end of the wedding table, he uses his telekinetic powers to kill Ahmed by lifting a fork from the table and directing it with his eyes in a deadly flight into the Sheikh's neck. He then stabs one of the brothers and almost manages to escape but is gunned down near the railway tracks.

The film concludes with a scene from the vigil around Perhan's coffin back home. The family is together – grandmother, sister, uncle and little son. Golden coins are placed over Perhan's eyes in the coffin. The mischievous little boy steals the coins and runs away. Even though ending with a death, the film closes in a playful mood.

*　　*　　*

One of the critics of *Father* had been that the film was too 'literary' and was making little use of purely cinematic devices in translating the script onto the screen. In *Gypsies* this is no longer the case. This time Kusturica had made a very cinematic film, which brought a profound change in his style and marked the beginning of his experimentation with magical realism.

Like the previous films, *Gypsies* also followed a linear narrative. The magic realist effect was achieved by the introduction of specific narrative elements (dream sequences, fantastic visions, telekinesis, levitation) and by the increased attention to camera style (complexly staged scenes, long elaborately choreographed takes). Fantastic single-take scenes, like the conversation of Perhan and Azra, first seen in front of a tall limestone oven, then as the camera moves up appearing on its very top and then as the camera moves back down seen again in front of the oven, are indeed extremely cinematic. Densely populated and dynamically evolving mass scenes replace the close plans of *Father*. While the specific use of colour spots is consistent with his earlier work, the director also develops new stylistic devices that will be represented in his subsequent films, like the binary narrative techniques that coordinate the scenes around vertical and horizontal, above and below, indoors and outdoors. Tarkovsky and Fellini, as seen particularly in the complex staging of some long takes, directly influence the camera work and the *mise-en-scène*. The musical score also plays an impor-

'Ederlezi' (the St George's Day celebration song) is the key scene in
Time of the Gypsies

tant part, particularly the choral arrangement of *Ederlezi*, which superbly
enhances the effect of all the key scenes of the film – the lovemaking dream
sequence, Azra's labour and death, and Perhan's death.

Here we also discover the widest range of cinematic 'make-overs' – a specific of Kusturica's style that consists of taking existing scenes from other films
and re-making them in the context of his own. 'In the middle of the shooting,'
the director said, ' I became very frightened when I realized I was doing both
Buñuel and John Ford and Buñuel and John Ford cannot go together!'
(Thomas, 1990, p. 6). In addition, for this film he also made over scenes from
films by Fellini, de Sica, Leone, Tarkovsky, Tati, Hanak and Menzel.

The film combines rough realism with fantasy elements. On the one
hand, there are the realistic depictions of everyday life and a high degree of
ethnographic authenticity. And the realistic characters – the gambling little
uncle who was better off as a *Gastarbeiter* in Germany, Azra's ambitious
mother who wants to profit from her fair-skinned daughter, or the

unscrupulous and corrupt crime lord, Ahmed, making a living in transnational trafficking. On the other hand, there is the added dimension of quasi-magical elements: the charm-healing abilities of the grandmother, Perhan's telekinesis and restless dreams.

Gypsies is one of the rare films shot almost exclusively in the vernacular Romani language, thus giving recognition of the Romani culture and mythology. It had to be subtitled in every country where it played. At the time of its release it encountered criticism from Roma in France and elsewhere for recycling all the negative social stereotypes associated with the Gypsies. Other Roma, however, have spoken of it as a truthful depiction of their difficult life experiences. The film undoubtedly helped to increase the visibility of the group and effectively furthered the appreciation of social issues affecting the Romani population in Yugoslavia.

In the press kit for the film Kusturica said that the Gypsies were 'the only ones inclined to associate the most important moments of their lives with the collective unconscious'. This is why he felt it appropriate that their experiences should be 'expressed through their dreams and imagination' (Thomas, 1990, p. 6). Such views, however, put Kusturica in the range of those writers and directors who have created and maintained the romanticised image of the Gypsy. Like them, he believes that the Romani experience is characterised by a frame of reference that transcends concrete social frameworks and ultimately dwells in a fantasy world. Thus, he also subscribes to the widely held belief that Roma are people without a sense of history who live in a timeless universe. Some of the most striking images of this otherwise realistic film seem to corroborate such a view: the house that is lifted and left hanging in the rain in the middle of the night suggests an absence of permanence and an overall volatility; the Gypsy settlement located amidst ancient Roman ruins suggests a harmonious coexistence with a long-forgotten past, one that is only possible for those who are outside the conventional framework of time and history.

Time of the Gypsies won the award for best direction at Cannes in 1989. This acclaimed film finally established Kusturica's reputation as a leading European auteur with influential film critics and art-house audiences. The reception was overwhelmingly positive and today the film is considered to represent magic realist film-making at its best. The theatrical release in America was delayed by the premature departure of David Puttnam from Columbia Pictures, which caused the film to be touted as one of 'Puttnam's orphans'. Ironically, here the film was rated R (restricted) for its 'violence, nudity and profanity'. American critics gave it polite applause, speaking highly of the style and the fantasy elements but expressing reservations about the ponderous narrative.

Arizona Dream (1993)

While teaching at Columbia, Kusturica became interested in a script by one of his students, David Atkins. It is difficult to judge what the original script might have looked like: there are indications that it was closer to an action film, evolving around crime and including shoot-outs – but no such elements were present in the completed film. As usual, Kusturica participated in the script development; both he and Atkins are credited as authors of the story, but only Atkins is credited as the screenwriter. Kusturica said the film was inspired by Salinger's *Catcher in the Rye* and he wanted it to be a film about suicide and about the American Dream.

Arizona Dream is an interesting case of a European, mostly French-backed, production, made in the US with some American involvement. Under the working title *Arrowtooth Waltz*, shooting took place in New York, Alaska and Douglas, Arizona, mostly in 1991. For the first time Kusturica worked with a cast of well-known Western actors – Johnny Depp, Faye Dunaway, Jerry Lewis and independent icons Lili Taylor and Vincent Gallo. In an interview Kusturica said the budget for the film was $15 million (Göttler, 1993). It does not look like an expensive production, but the originally allocated budget was exceeded, leading to a bitter showdown between the director and the American partners.

The opening scenes take place in Alaska. An Eskimo who has caught a big flat fish nearly dies in a snowstorm. He is rescued by his dogs and revived in his igloo by his wife. The Eskimo couple want to be alone, so they give their child a balloon and send him out. The red balloon is released in the air. It travels all over America until it reaches Manhattan and descends over Central Park and the Hudson River.

The balloon lands on the open back of a truck where the film's protagonist, Axel Blackmar, has just woken up. Axel is introduced in his own voice-
over. He is originally from the Southwest near the Mexican border; he lost
his parents in a car accident, for which his Uncle Leo seems to have been
responsible. Axel, who is now twenty-three and still a dreamer, works for
the Department of Fisheries in New York.

Uncle Leo, a Cadillac dealer in a small Arizona town, is getting married.
He wants Axel to be his best man and has sent Paul, a childhood friend, to
fetch him from New York. Axel resists, but Paul gets him drunk and abducts
him. When Axel comes to his senses, it is too late, as they are near their destination, surrounded by Arizona's desert-like landscape, full of eccentrics
and Cadillacs. The town is a typical Southwest outpost, with deserted, sun-
baked streets and ugly, rectangular buildings with wide spaces in-between.

Leo Sweetie, the uncle, presides over a glossy Cadillac empire, lives in a
house painted in sugary pink and wears matching suits and bolo ties. He is
about to marry a young immigrant woman half his age, whom he describes
as 'my Polish cup cake'. Because America is all about success and success
means selling cars, Leo is determined to make Axel an associate and possibly have him take over the Cadillac business. Axel is not too excited by these
plans, but agrees to stay on for a few days until the wedding. Leo projects a
home movie of Axel's childhood.

At the dealership Axel meets local beauty Elaine Stalker, a rich widow, and
her step-daughter Grace. Both Axel and Paul are attracted to Elaine, blonde
and gorgeous and they soon end up at a dinner party in their place. At dinner
they all talk of their dreams: Axel of Alaska and a flat fish that has both eyes on
the same side; Elaine of Papua-New Guinea and flying; and Grace of turtles,
suicide and reincarnation. Amid the exotic and insane atmosphere of the
dinner Axel falls in love with Elaine so madly that he simply stays over. Their
mutual attraction is based on exciting sex, mostly hinted at rather than
shown, as well as on Axel's fascination with Elaine's dream of flying (like an
Icarus, she keeps falling down each time). When they are not in bed, Axel
spends his time working on devices that would help Elaine fly, devices that
grow increasingly complex but nonetheless fail to work. A mysterious flying
fish appears in Axel's dreams and turns his contraptions into wrecks.

Axel's flying devices grow increasingly complex but nonetheless fail to work

Uncle Leo is unhappy with Axel's involvement with Elaine, who is much older and comes to claim him back. But he has no luck. After a confrontation with Elaine, who chases him with a rifle, Leo runs away. Axel and Elaine stay at the house, a remote ranch in the middle of a valley surrounded by blue mountain ranges.

Grace has been an annoying presence throughout. She hates her stepmother whom she blames for the death of her father. She won't leave the lovers alone, hysterically playing the accordion and obsessively manifesting her suicidal intentions. There is plenty of tension between her and Axel. It gets so bad that one night Axel takes a gun to Grace's bedroom with the apparent intention of getting rid of her. But Grace is not afraid; she seems to have been waiting for him. She challenges Axel to play Russian roulette, which they both survive even though some shots are produced.

While attending a talent audition where his friend Paul is performing the crop-dusting plane chase scene from Hitchcock's *North by Northwest*, Axel is urgently called to Leo's. Shortly thereafter the uncle dies in Axel's presence, in an ambulance heading towards the hospital; it looks like a heart attack but is more likely a suicide. In a magic realist twist, the ambulance takes off and flies to the moon.

Axel has taken some time off to recover from the trauma of Leo's death. When he returns to Elaine's, they have an argument. Axel has bought a small plane for Elaine's birthday from his inheritance. She can finally fly and excitedly does so around the ranch, chasing Paul in scenes replicating his *North by Northwest* performance. Axel and Grace grow closer and seem to fall in love. During the party that evening, with a Mariachi band, a piñata and gifts in front of the fireplace, their bond gets even stronger. Axel, however, ends up in Elaine's bedroom where they are shown having a heated argument. Meanwhile Grace, who has retreated and waits for Axel in a bridal dress, walks out in the rain and shoots herself before he manages to interfere. It all happens in the midst of a thunderstorm. Lightning strikes the tree in front of the house and burns it down.

In the epilogue Leo and Axel are seen line fishing in Alaska. Their conversation, carried out in Eskimo, evolves around metaphors of maturity. It is all about Axel's coming of age, a new status that he now seems ready to accept.

*   *   *

Arizona is a film that summarises Kusturica's interest in America. First and foremost, there is his fascination with the diversity of extreme locations that are brought together: Alaska, New York and the Southwest. But the film, Kusturica said, was also meant to feature everything he hated while living in America (Elhem, 1993, p.19). He wanted to parody the kitsch and the Cadillac culture and considered using the title 'I Even Met Unhappy Americans' (paraphrasing the title of Aleksandar Petrović's Yugoslav film classic), to scrutinise the annoying American ideology of 'achievers' by focusing on the losers.

The film was released after substantial cuts and this cutting may partially account for a certain incoherence of the narrative. The protagonists are not losers (as the director has called them), but eccentrics. Suicide is supposed to be one of the leading themes, as well as daydreaming, but they are never investigated deeply enough. The unconvincing dramatic build-ups are most clearly felt in some of Axel's moves – like his decision to kill Grace. Axel may be 'flying in love', but Johnny Depp's performance is not really electrifying. Could it be the actor? Around the same time Depp starred in Lasse Hallström's *What's Eating Gilbert Grape* (1993), a film about real losers and was perfectly convincing.

But *Arizona Dream* marks some important developments in Kusturica's style, all of which are at odds with mainstream Hollywood ideas of cinema. First of all, he has done a lot to achieve a faster pacing, mostly via editing. As with any European film-maker confronted with Americans, he must have heard a lot from his students at Columbia about the off-puttingly slow pace of East European films. Nonetheless, the film remains quite slow due to the convoluted plotline that no editing can remedy. Second, the film-maker neglects basic American rules of dramaturgy such as audience identification with the protagonist, clear-cut motivation in character development and a dramatic build-up leading to a pay-off at the end. Third, genre conventions are ignored: *Arizona* is not a drama, not a romantic comedy, not a thriller, nor an action or a Western, nor a family saga or a melodrama. It subverts the concept of genre by combining elements of all genres.

The film contains some magic realist elements – dream sequences featuring the flat flying fish and an ambulance taking off to the moon – but they do not have a key role in the narrative. At the same time, important narrative elements – the defining role of location, the quest for extreme places like Arizona and Alaska – remain insufficiently developed. As in *Time of the Gypsies*, a haunting score of choral folk singing accompanies all death scenes.

There are also all the 'homages' that Kusturica pays to American films. *Arizona Dream* contains references to, among others, Welles' *The Lady from Shanghai* (1948), Bogdanovich's *Last Picture Show* (1971), Penn's *Bonnie and Clyde* (1967), Altman's *Brewster McCloud* (1970), Coppola's *Godfather II*, Scorsese's *Taxi Driver* and *Raging Bull* (1980), Cox's *Repo Man* (1984), Spielberg's *E.T.* (1982), Cimino's *Deer Hunter* (1978), Wenders' *Paris, Texas* (1984) and van Sant's *My Own Private Idaho* (1991). Further references are found in the names, such as the waitress Blanche (like the protagonist of Kazan's *Streetcar Named Desire* [1951]), Leo Sweetie (like Jane Campion's *Sweetie* [1989]) and Elaine Stalker (like Tarkovsky's *Stalker* [1979]). Besides a 'make-over' of the burning tree from *Offret* (*Sacrifice*, 1986), Tarkovsky's work is made over in scenes involving windows and rain. It all comes backed up by an image inventory of quintessential American objects, such as ceiling fans, pink Cadillacs, plastic flamingoes and neon cactuses.

The film had a fairly cold reception in America. The *New York Times'* Janet Maslin, for example, described it as a 'slapstick psychodrama with a heavy dash of magical realism', and as a 'fish out of water' (1995, p. 13). In Europe, however, *Arizona Dream* acquired some sort of cult status and many in Eastern Europe just loved it, maybe because it corresponded to their vision of the American Dream.

Underground (1995)

For *Underground (Podzemlje: Bila jednom jedna zemlja/There Was Once a Land)* Kusturica collaborated with Dušan Kovačević, a leading Yugoslav playwright. Once again, scriptwriter and director worked closely, and the script is credited to both. It is based on Kovačević's earlier plays, but also uses motives of a popular Yugoslav TV series from the 1970s, *Otpisani (Written Off)*, about the adventures of two accidental resistance fighters.

Initially, the director approached the film as a 'surrealist comedy that will allow me to keep my sanity' (Ciment, 1993, p. 25). Yet another reason for making the film was, in his words, that he had 'enough of these western humanists who play with ideologies by going to Yugoslavia and by using the Bosnian situation for strengthening their market image' (Ostria, 1994, p. 78). Kusturica felt it was important he make a statement on Yugoslavia's break-up. The final result was a historical film rich in metaphors intended to give insights into the violent state of affairs in Yugoslavia in the 1990s.

Underground had a composite budget, coming from a variety of sources, especially France, Germany and Hungary, and with the financial participation of such funding bodies as Eurimages, as well as the involvement of Czech studio Barrandov, the Yugoslav production company Komuna, Radio-Television Serbia and the Bulgarian Chapline Films. This is the last Kusturica film shot by his permanent cameraman, Vilko Filač, with whom he had a relationship based on mutual confidence and intuitive understanding developed during their fifteen years of collaboration.

The film's narrative spans over five decades, highlighting episodes taking place in 1941, 1961 and 1992. Real events are combined with fictional historical encounters and occurrences. Documentary footage of selected moments of Yugoslav history is used as a background on which the fictional protagonists mingle with real historical personalities as seen in Woody Allen's *Zelig* (1983) and Robert Zemeckis's *Forrest Gump* (1994). Elaborate *mise-en-scène*, dark colours, ornate props and a haunting musical score create the film's unique atmosphere and rhythm, leaving a lasting and unsettling impression.

The film follows three protagonists – Marko Dren (Miki Manojlović), a manipulative cynic, Petar Popara-Blacky (Lazar Ristovski), a simpleton strongman and Natalija Zvonko (Mirjana Joković), an opportunistic starlet – whose lives intersect with select moments of Yugoslav history. Marko and Blacky both fall for Natalija and many of their actions are determined by their romantic rivalry. The sombre backdrop to these affairs of the heart is a war with no end and the three parts of the film are respectively called 'War', 'Cold War' and 'War'.

In the first part, which opens with the Nazi bombing of Belgrade in 1941, Marko, an energetic black-marketeer, takes a group of friends and relatives, including his brother, the zoo-keeper Ivan (Slavko Štimac) and Blacky's pregnant wife Vera (Mirjana Karanović), to a cellar which he has equipped as an air-raid shelter. Blacky's son, Jovan, is born in the cellar; the mother dies at birth. Documentary footage shows people in Slovenia and Croatia cheering at the arrival of the Nazis, juxtaposed with footage of destruction and gloom in Belgrade.

It soon turns out that the whole rescue operation was planned by Marko with the intention of enslaving the people in the cellar. Above ground, Marko and Blacky complete a series of reckless robberies and protection rackets that they present as motivated by anti-fascist zeal. Three years pass. Natalija, an actress at the National Theatre, is involved with a Nazi officer. Blacky performs a daring stunt and abducts her from the stage to a ship on the Danube where they are to be married. On the ship Marko confesses his affection for Natalija, but she is soon reunited with her German lover. Blacky is arrested and tortured. In a manifestation of his philanderer's showmanship, Marko arranges a jailbreak for Blacky and kills Natalija's Nazi lover. He takes Natalija and her handicapped brother Bato to his house and sends the liberated Blacky to 'hide' in the cellar, thus effectively getting rid of him. He can finally claim Natalija exclusively for himself. Belgrade is bombed once again, this time by the Allied forces.

The events of the second part, 'Cold War', take place in 1961. In communist Yugoslavia, Marko has become a celebrated poet, close to President Tito. He has married Natalija and together they have created a mythology of their wartime experiences as brave anti-fascists. A film is to be shot about their heroic experiences in the struggle. Simultaneously, Marko still keeps a large number of people, Blacky included, in the cellar. He tricks the cellar inhabitants into believing that the war is still going on by playing soundtracks of Nazi bombings and Hitler's speeches, while using them as slave labour to manufacture arms that are traded internationally. It is an ongoing show that Marko maintains with a variety of stage devices. He even smears himself with mud and tears his clothes to pretend he was tortured by the Gestapo.

Though not an important element of the plot, the kiss of the flying bride remains one of the most memorable scenes in *Underground*

One day Marko and Natalija go down to the cellar to attend the wedding of Blacky's son Jovan. Sweaty drunkenness reigns over this claustrophobic celebration and the wedding guests, all intoxicated, end up in a brawl. Marko is challenged by Blacky and pretends to pull the trigger on himself, while in fact only injuring his leg. In the turmoil, the walls of the cellar crumble. The members of the wedding disperse in disarray, discovering an elaborate system of tunnels that links the major European capitals and carries a lively underground traffic. Blacky and Jovan climb above ground and end up at the shooting site of the film based on Marko's memoirs of the 'revolutionary' struggle of the fearless threesome, supposed to glorify Blacky's own heroic past. Mistaking the set for reality and believing that World War II is still going on, Blacky and his son kill all the actors wearing German uniforms. At sunrise, Jovan, incapable of living outside the cellar, drowns in the Danube. The police capture Blacky. Marko and Natalija blow up the house and the cellar and escape. Signs inform us that the disappearance of Marko Dren

Kusturica casts himself in a cameo as a Bosnian dunce who is sent on a mission to purchase arms

made Comrade Tito so ill, that he died twenty years later. This part ends with documentary footage of Tito's funeral, with a range of international political celebrities in attendance.

The narrative makes a thirty-year jump, from 1961 to 1992, a time span exceeding the existence of the Berlin wall (1961–89), the symbol of communism in Europe. The third part, again called 'War', is set in the 1990s at an unidentified battlefield, presumably Eastern Slavonia, where the protagonists' paths cross one last time. Blacky, still mourning the loss of his son thirty-odd years earlier, is now in command of paramilitary forces shelling a nearby city. A wheelchair-confined Marko and his devoted wife Natalija have become major figures in international arms sales and are wanted by Interpol. Protected by UN soldiers in blue helmets, they negotiate an arms sale with a Bosnian.

Ivan, Marko's brother, has lived in a psychiatric hospital in Berlin ever since escaping from the cellar. Back on Yugoslav soil now, he has finally realised Marko's betrayal. In a final showdown, he encounters Marko near the battlefield and beats him to death, then commits suicide. A paratrooper shoots Natalija. Marko and Natalija's bodies are set on fire and left in the wheelchair to turn around an inverted crucifix in the centre of a small square. Blacky passes by and recognises his former friends, but it is too late to interfere.

The film's epilogue offers a sharp contrast to this apocalyptic closure. In a utopian wedding scene, Jovan and Jelena's underground wedding is replayed once again. It is an imaginary one, set on the Danube's sunny shore. The Romani brass band play as guests gather from all sides – the same people that betrayed and fought each other for the duration of the film now come back to life. In contrast to the darkness of the underground here the sun shines and all are cheerful, embracing each other and dancing in oblivion. Ivan, Marko's brother, turns to the camera and addresses the viewers:

> Here, we built new houses with red roofs and opened the doors widely to welcome cherished guests. And we are grateful to the land for feeding us. And grateful to the sun for shining on us. In pain, sadness and joy, we still remember our country. And we will tell our children this tale of our home: once upon a time there was a country …

While the celebration goes on, the piece of land where they stand breaks apart from the mainland and quietly floats away. The wedding guests are too busy dancing and singing to notice that they are being carried away to an unknown destination.

*   *   *

Underground was conceived and shot following an extended script, and from the outset it was clear that the result would be a film much longer than the standard hour-and-a-half — two hours, in fact. A look at the long version (which Kusturica edited for Serbian television) gives important insights into the director's intentions before the film was cut down for international theatrical use.

Some subplots, like an adventure featuring Marko disguised in a bridal dress abducting a train full of firearms, do not make much difference to the film's reading. But there are two important plotlines that need to be looked at.

First of all, there are substantial cuts related to plotlines that involve Natalija. In the longer version of the film, she is granted an extensive presence allowing for a better understanding and justification of her motives. It is her concern for the well-being of her handicapped brother Bato that determines many of her opportunistic actions. While in the cinema version Bato disappears in 1944, in the long version he lives in an attic room at Marko and Natalija's house until 1961 and is the person responsible for the manipulative broadcasts maintaining the impression that war is still going on. Another thing that is lost in the shorter version is Natalija's consistent contempt for Marko. Their relationship is tense and abusive — there is an extended scene in the long version showing Marko raping Natalija, a climax in the long line of his routine blackmail of her. None of these scenes have made it to the short version, where Natalija's character comes across as an implausible cross between Eva Peron and Elena Ceausescu. The scene in which Natalija performs an erotic dance with the tank's muzzle, however, has stayed and made for a good promotional image used in catalogues and press stills.

The other aspect of the long version that has been significantly downplayed in the short version are the plotlines that give a clearer idea of the

Natalija's erotic dance with the tank's muzzle made for a good promotional image

film's underlying views on national character and geopolitics. Several characters that only have an episodic presence in the short version play an important role here – the Bosnian Mustafa, the Slovene Janez and the Croatian Tomislav – who are all involved with Marko and Blacky's criminal activities at the time of World War II. After the war they are shown gradually prospering on the shadowy side of domestic politics and becoming gangsters of international stature. It is they who actually run the sinister arms trade during the Cold War period. Marko's actions are often shown as dictated by his association with them, a damaging bondage he cannot escape.

Last but not least, the long version of the film also includes a satirical take on German attitudes: just before Ivan's escape from a Berlin hospital where he has spent thirty years, he is demonstrated to medical students as a representative *Homo balkanicus*. The German professor explains his theories of the idiosyncratic genetic and cultural roots of this Balkan specimen by moving his pointer all over Ivan's body.

The material that was cut from the theatrical version made it to a TV series shown in Serbia in 1995 and served as the basis of the long version of *Underground* that was broadcast in France and released on video in 1998.

Stylistically, *Underground* was particularly impressive. The masterful camera work made the best of dark colours and of the extensive use of the circle as a basic visual element, achieved through a variety of panning, revolving and turning shots meant to show the characters' voyage through the circles of hell. The imaginative sets made the film's fantastic spaces habitable and the music was crucial for maintaining its rhythm. As in his other films, here Kusturica 'quoted' not only various examples of *film noir* and Vigo's *L'Atalante* (1934), but also Welles' *The Stranger* (1946), Reed's *The Third Man* (1949), Wajda's *Kanal* (1957) and *Popiól i diament* (*Ashes and Diamonds*, 1958), Tarkovsky's *Ivanovo detstvo* (*My Name is Ivan*, 1962), as well as films by Leone, Coppola, Gilliam and others.

Magic realist elements are scarce in this film, replaced by a somewhat frivolous use of historical time and the insertion of fictional characters into historical footage. Some of the extensive and lavish scenes (a wedding on a ship, the wedding in the cellar) do not appear important from the point of view of narrative development, but have a display value that the director deliberately sought. He was mostly preoccupied with aesthetic categories such as the baroque and the spectacular and moral categories such as betrayal and commitment.

At the 1995 Cannes International Film Festival *Underground* (theatrical version) was awarded the Palme d'Or, adding to Kusturica's previous awards and strengthening the director's reputation as a 'Balkan Fellini'. Some reviews hailed the film as a great intellectual achievement, making references to Plato's cave, Dante's descent into the circles of hell, Hegel's dialectics and Jung's collective unconscious. Others classified it as an eso-teric piece of elitist cinema preoccupied with the messy state of Balkan affairs and gave it a lukewarm reception, summarised by Derek Malcolm's statement that the film certainly 'is extraordinary, but I'm not sure whether it is extraordinarily good or extraordinarily bad' (Malcolm, 1995, p. 10).

Many wondered what Kusturica thought of Yugoslavia, for which the film was supposed to be a metaphor. The director had revealed publicly that the Union of South Slavs had been an artificial political construction built on lies and mutual betrayal. But the Yugonostalgic'epilogue suggested that he was mourning for this same deceptive appearance of togetherness, even though he subverted it in the course of the film's narrative. Tony Rayns' perceptive comment was probably the best critique of *Underground*: 'The film's real political problem is not that it fails to be "correctly" partisan but that it rests on nostalgia for a national identity which it simultaneously exposes as a skillfully manipulated illusion' (1996, p. 53).

Crna mačka, beli mačor (Black Cat, White Cat, 1998)

Crna mačka, beli mačor was originally conceived as a documentary about the Romani musicians who participated in *Underground*. At some point the pro-ject changed from a documentary to a feature short and then to a full-length feature. The film was scripted by Gordan Mihić of *Gypsies*, who used a range of Gypsy stories, as well as motives from a short story by Isaac Babel, which was proposed by Kusturica and on which Dadan's character was loosely based. *Black Cat* was co-produced by CiBY (France), Pandora (Germany) and Komuna (Yugoslavia) and was shot on the Danube, near Belgrade, over two summers. The financing was an international affair, with mostly French and German contributions and Yugoslav participation. In a 1999 interview Kusturica quoted a $4.5 million-dollar budget. For this film, there were important changes in Kusturica's crew, with new key team members replac-ing the old regulars. The mechanical contraptions of set designer Kreka are no longer there but the protagonists move around assisted by similarly awe-some mechanical devices, created by Milenko Jeremić. The elegance of

Vilko Filač's camera is no longer there but the camera style of Frenchmen Thierry Arbogast (a regular worker with André Techiné and Luc Besson) and Michel Amathieu is proficient and dynamic. The striking musical arrangements of Goran Bregović are no longer there but the frantic score by the 'new primitive' Dr Nele Karajilić efficiently maintains the film's rhythm. As far as the cast is concerned, the film employs some of Kusturica's regulars from *Gypsies* (Ljubica Adžović, Zabit Memedov, Irfan Jagli) and *Underground*, but also new faces, like Sabri Sulejman (the flamboyant Gypsy baron Grga Pitić). The director has taken special pride in his ability to work with non-professional Romani actors, whom he has often described as mostly illiterate, requiring a special approach (which he compares to Madeleine Albright's) to keep their loyalty: 'One day, I threaten the Gypsies, the other day, I am their best friend' (Kaufman, 1999).

The film runs over two hours and juggles numerous plotlines of mutual betrayals and conspiracies combined in a narrative that frequently comes close to falling apart. Unlike Kusturica's other films, the story in *Black Cat* is not the most important thing. Plotlines in this film derive from the film-maker's interest in including certain trademark scenes; the stories are adjusted to assist him in fully using his idiosyncratic imagery and imagination.

There are roughly five plotlines evolving around the life of a Gypsy community scattered along the shore of the Danube:

1. Matko is a constantly failing Gyspy entrepreneur living in a shack on the Danube with his son, the teenage Zare. Once again betrayed by smugglers, he borrows even more under false pretences. He gets involved with Dadan (played by Srdjan Todorović, who was Jovan in *Underground*), a Gypsy gangster, who also betrays him while smuggling a cargo train full of petrol at the Bulgarian border. On top of this, Dadan blackmails Matko into agreeing to marry off Zare to Dadan's sister, a midget called Afrodita (Ladybird). Matko reluctantly agrees.

2. Zare, Matko's son, is in love with Ida, a blonde Gypsy. They make love in a sunflower field. The idyll, however, is shadowed by the revelations that pre-arranged marriages are planned for both of them. They are determined to resist.

3. Dadan is a curly haired, coke-sniffing and gold-chain-wearing prosperous Gypsy gangster. He wears white suits, bosses everyone around and gambles incessantly. He lives in conspicuous wealth and rides in a chauffeur-driven limousine surrounded by girls and bodyguards. His only concern is his three sisters. The two older ones he has already married off, even though they are ugly. Now is the turn of Afrodita, the midget. She resists the marriage arrangement, but is coerced into it by Dadan and his bodyguards. At the wedding, Afrodita escapes and runs away. Dadan and the others chase her.

4. In an attempt to prevent the unwanted marriage of Zare and Afrodita, Zare's grandfather pretends to die. But the wedding is not postponed; the grandfather's body is tucked away in the attic and cooled down with the help of a large chunk of ice. Grga Pitić, an extravagant Gypsy lord, lives in a compound, moves around in exotic vehicles, wears huge silver teeth and black mirror glasses and endlessly replays the ending of his favourite film, *Casablanca* (1942). He comes to the wedding in his capacity as a family friend, but shortly after his arrival he has a heart attack and is believed dead, so his body, along with another ice block, is also tucked away in the attic.

5. Grga Pitić Jr., Grga's seven-foot-tall grandson, is under pressure to marry but he has not yet met a girl he likes. In the middle of a forest he comes across Afrodita running away from her wedding. Theirs is love at first glance.

The ending is happy for all. The dead grandfathers come back to life. Dadan is punished. Afrodita is married to Grga Jr. and Ida to Zare. Love triumphs.

These main plots coexist with numerous extraneous subplots – a dead customs officer's body hangs on a barrier near a railway crossing, a huge singer deploys her butt to take nails out of a plank, a drunken official messes up the wedding ceremony – all adding to the picture's exuberance and merrymaking. In addition, fairy-tale elements (a bride turning into a bird, a giant and a midget, two ugly older sisters, a shoe lost on the run) and elements of the post-communist folklore (Russian army paraphernalia, underground whisky brewing and green-haired bodyguards), are used throughout. But

In *Black Cat, White Cat*, the director comes across as a committed image-maker

the mutual attraction of opposites is only one dimension. The narrative is constructed around doubles and duality: there are two weddings, two grand-fathers and, of course, two cats. To Michele Marangi, the synthesis of oppo-sites, present in Kusturica's work from early on, is brought to completion in this film. Like the two supplementary halves of the Yin and Yang circle, here Matko (black clothes) is supplemented by Dadan (white suit) and the big groom finds his little bride (Boni, 1999, pp. 139–49). Kusturica's definition of 'joy' as a combination of 'happiness' and 'sorrow', is brought to comple-tion in this film.

Black Cat is the film that best represents the director's mature style bringing together all the elements he has been developing since 1988. There was no
chance that this film would be accused of being 'too literary'. On the contrary,
this time *Cahiers du cinéma* declared it 'too cinematic'. Very little of the early
Kusturica is left here. Close-ups are no longer used as windows into someone's soul but mostly to show faces we are to marvel at. The protagonists are no
longer there to care about but mostly to admire for being so extraordinarily
exotic. The plotlines are no longer well-matched jigsaw pieces but mostly
fantasies of love and death that intersect and cross paths but never quite come
together. Things are happening all the time, at all levels and in all corners. The
white and red spots are still there, but this time with a number of other
coloured spots added, most notably blue, but also yellow, pink, green and dark
orange. Even though the recycling of Vigo, Fellini and Tarkovsky continues,
with added references ranging from Dovzhenko to Kaurismäki, the film is
dominated by a trademark taste for trashy popular culture as seen in the
spaghetti Western and in the work of Tarantino and Almodovar.

While thematically *Black Cat* is also a 'Gypsy' film, here Kusturica's
approach to the Roma is radically different. Neither the authenticity nor the
magic realism of *Gypsies* remain. Instead, the Romani existence is presented
as a feel-good roller-coaster adventure, plunging viewers into dizzy
escapades of thrilling protagonists, all involved in swindling, smuggling
and passionate dancing at weddings. It is a microcosm of exuberant flam-
boyance, populated by freewheeling creatures bathing in sunshine and
making love amidst sunflowers. A lifestyle so excitingly contagious that a
hospitalised Gypsy grandfather jumps out of his bed and leaves the ward on
a dancing step at the first sounds of the Romani band.

Everybody in *Black Cat* appears overtaken by the same intense vigour and
desire for life. No place for melancholy or squalor remains. Poverty or social
exclusion is irrelevant and all the protagonists live in a self-contained
universe of celebratory enjoyment. The Romani population of Yugoslavia
today may still have the same problems as it had at the time of *Gypsies*, it may
still be poverty-ridden and exposed to racist attacks. But ten years on these
concerns are no longer of interest to Kusturica. He finds it more appropriate
to focus on the towering kitsch of Grga Pitić's conspicuous wealth or the

overwhelming intensity of Dadan's suspicious affairs. While *Gypsies* had memorable characters, *Black Cat* is built on memorable caricatures.

Black Cat invites a re-examination of the director's interest in the Roma. Back in 1989, when he presented Romani experiences through the use of symbolism and magic elements, he was motivated by a social concern over the causes of trafficking and marginalisation. Ten years on, his interest comes across as purely aesthetic, mostly pursuing the creation of a rich and exotic image inventory.

Enjoyable to watch and apolitical, this film is probably the widest-seen and reviewed Kusturica film so far. While it did not further the director's career, it reasserted his reputation as a man capable of making feel-good pictures that do not seem to offend anyone, provided Romani critics were not loud enough to make themselves heard regarding the film's overt exploitation and exoticisation of Gypsies. Ironically, the movie premiered internationally at the time when NATO was bombing the very places on the Danube where the film was shot, forcing the director to give angry interviews condemning the aggression.

The critics received *Black Cat* relatively well, even though some admitted that they found the Gypsy exoticism over-the-top. The reaction to the film could be summarised in Dave Kehr's review, which even though written for *Time of the Gypsies* nearly a decade earlier (1990, p. 7) could have easily been re-used for *Black Cat*:

> Kusturica pushes all of his effects to a mad extreme. His grotesque is super-grotesque, his cute is super-cute and (most painfully) his noisy and crowded, super-noisy and super-crowded. Although one glimpses into an intriguingly different, underground Europe, the movie finally seems to leave its real-world references behind, feeding on its own extravagant imagery and relentless rhythms. It's as if the director, overwhelmed by all the cash at his disposal, had begun to hyperventilate.

Other works

In 1996 Kusturica made a politically suggestive short for France 2, *Sept jours dans la vie d'un oiseau* (*Seven Days in the Life of a Bird*), the story of

The mise-en-scène in *When Father Was Away on Business* (1985)
resembles the work of the Czech New Wave

When Father Was Away on Business

The neighbour's boy in *When Father Was Away on Business* tries to break a chain with his chest, like Zampanò in Fellini's *La Strada* (1954)

The face of the 'leader' (Tito/Mussolini) used as a background for rituals performed by organised children's groups, as seen in Kusturica's *When Father Was Away on Business*, top, and Fellini's *Amarcord* (1974), bottom

Scenes where water is poured over the head – here Muzafer's in *When Father Was Away on Business* – are influenced by Tarkovsky's treatment of water in *Mirror* (1975)

Jean Vigo's *L'Atalante* (1934) inspires this image from *Underground* (1995)

The wedding in *When Father Was Away on Business*, top, is set up in a way that is reminiscent of Fellini's *Amarcord*, bottom

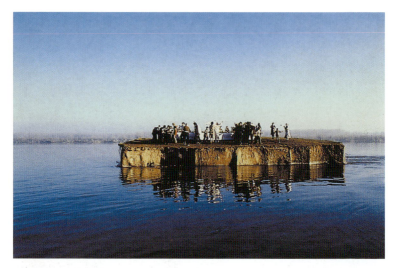

Underground (1995)

Kusturica's expressive faces are like those of Sergio Leone: Sabri Sulejman as Grga Pitic in *Black Cat, White Cat* (1998) resembles one of Leone's bandits

No Smoking Orchestra

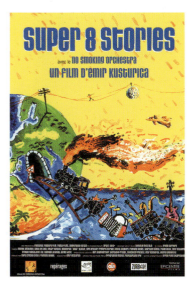

Poster for *Super 8 Stories* (2001)

Red spot in *Time of the Gypsies* (1989)

a Serb who cannot leave his house without trespassing on his neighbours' land and who dreams of turning into a bird. In Germany in 1997 he made an ad for an AIDS campaign that created controversy, as it failed to recommend the use of condoms. Kusturica has also made advertising spots in France – for cigarettes, XS perfume, La Banque Populaire and, more recently, for Renault. In his 2001 interview for the Yugoslav magazine *NIN* he said he mostly lives from filming commercials and music videos.

Super 8 Stories (2001)

An international production involving funding from Italy and Germany and fourteen cinematographers (including Kusturica), this documentary was shot on digital video and Super 8 and then blown up to 35mm. It uses a range of archival material and home videos, as well as musical video clips. According to the promotional materials, the film is in pursuit of the origins of the 'frantic, irresistible music' that speaks of 'the wild, mad, creative, dramatic world of the Balkans' and is defined either as 'Balkan punk' or as 'Gypsy techno-rock'.

The film highlights the No Smoking Orchestra (www.emirkusturica-nosmoking.com), the band with which Kusturica has played off and on since 1986. Given that the use of his name is the main tool for the group's promotion and hyping up today, Kusturica keeps a surprisingly low profile in the film. The story of the band is told in fragments, mostly by its founder, Dr Nele Karajilić and supported by archival and home video footage. Karajilić stresses the band's politically active past: besides creating music with 'protest in mind', they were behind the daring political sketches *Surrealist's Top List* on Sarajevo television in the late 1980s and early 90s. Karajilić tells the camera he was subjected to a witch-hunt by Bosnian Muslim police and ended up in Belgrade where No Smoking Orchestra became a 'world band'. Touring internationally today, they liken themselves to a Gypsy caravan.

The black-and-white interviews, shot mainly by Kusturica in a *This is Spinal Tap* style, take place on a bus. They are intercut with black-and-white grainy footage of older home videos or re-enacted daily life situations. The members of the band are quite diverse, from the tuba player Aleksandar Balaban, a village musician from Republika Srpska, to the Belgrade saxophone player Nenad Petrović, a sophisticated urbanite. Together, the interviews with band members create an ethnography of today's Yugoslavia, with its Gypsy-music bars and destroyed bridges on the Danube. The best home video footage shows Kusturica in the 1980s playing in the snow with his son, Stribor, then a little boy but now a big 200-pound man and a drummer for the band.

Then there is the footage of the concerts, taken mostly at two venues in Berlin and Paris in 1999. With flashing lights and exhilarated audience, the performances are an eclectic crossover between The Sex Pistols, Iggy Pop and the Russian Nautilus Pompilius, led by Dr Nele who sings in barely comprehensible German or English, as well as in Serbian. Kusturica, in a straw hat and with a cigar hanging from his mouth, crosses the stage in a rhythmic walk

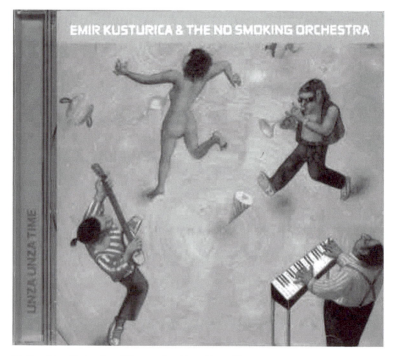

No Smoking Orchestra: CD cover for *Unza Unza Time*

reminiscent of scenes from *Reservoir Dogs* (1992). He talks to the audience, telling them about 'extra proteins' (also a topic for Axel in *Arizona Dream*) and repeating the *Casablanca* line that Grga Pitić addressed the audience with at the end of *Black Cat*: 'This is the beginning of a beautiful friendship!'

Extended attention is given to the roadshow's life behind the stage: Emir wrestling with son Stribor in the dressing room, the dislocated shoulder of guitarist Glava, a Polaroid photo shoot in an Italian palazzo peppered with boorish jokes and lots of booze everywhere. It is a macho universe where women appear either as torsos bumping at the hand-held camera that tracks the male protagonists, or as a shadowy presence behind windows.

All this is intercut with re-enactments, among which the musical clip of a number called *Unza Unza Time* stands out. Realised in hurried black-and-white scenes meant to imitate early silent films, the clip is set on an old-fashioned train and evolves around a range of familiar and new images (a bride, a handcar, a goat, a contrabass, a pair of dancing nuns).

Super 8 Stories is a first for Kusturica in many aspects: first documentary, first digital video, first-time extensive assemblage of diverse visual material. The director demonstrates remarkable skill in combining colour footage with grainy black and white, as well as in his selection and use of home video material. Without being excessively self-referential, the film features themes and images typical of his repertoire – mirrors, trains, brides and animals.

Super 8 Stories presents the No Smoking band as a major Yugoslav cultural export that subverts Western rock clichés, as a musical phenomenon. But this is not necessarily what the band means to everyone else. Much is said about No Smoking as they want to see themselves, but many topics are conveniently avoided under the disguise of apolitical music assemblage. The promotional materials claim that the musicians 'have not taken sides when passing through that region's tragedies', but it is a fact that its leading members, originally from Bosnia, ended up in Belgrade. The grainy footage of the destroyed bridges in Belgrade reveals the city as the present-day home of most band members. The footage of peaceful Sarajevo from before the war, with no trace of destruction, reveals it as a happy memory spot, a place with no real present-day meaning.

For a long time, Kusturica has been saying he prefers to be a musician because making music is a more fulfilling experience than film-making. For a long time he has been interested in shooting in digital video. For a long time he has wanted to make a film that would be easy and enjoyable to shoot and would give him a break from the emotionally exhausting involvement with serious film-making. And he has done it now, with *Super 8 Stories*, a film that is all fun and little else.

Projects

As an award-winning director, Kusturica has often been asked about his forthcoming plans. Such a question was not yet relevant at the time of *Dolly Bell*. But in the press kit for *Father* he was already said to be working on a film called *The Magpie Strategy*. There was no indication in what capacity he was involved, so it seemed normal to assume that he was set to direct. When the film materialised in 1987, however, a Bosnian production on a contemporary social topic, it was directed by Zlatko Lavanić, who worked as an assistant director on *Father*. Kusturica was only listed as a collaborator on the script.

Before resorting to work on *Gypsies*, he considered a theme proposed by his London-based producer, Harry Saltzman. *Dukhobors* (a.k.a. *The Spirit Wrestlers*) was supposed to take place in western Canada, amidst a group of old Orthodox believers. Kusturica seemed interested and even travelled to British Columbia, but then dropped the project. He opted instead to work on a film about Gypsies, a group that was closer to him and embodied 'everything that is archetypal and outright mystic, which is what I needed' (press kit for *Gypsies*).

Later on, around the time of *Arizona*, Kusturica was firmly committed to a project for a loose adaptation of *Crime and Punishment* that was to be shot in 16mm and was to star Johnny Depp. The film was supposed to be set in present-day Brighton Beach, the New York suburb inhabited predominantly by Russian immigrants, with a modern-day Raskolnikov playing a bass guitar in a band. In the early stages of his work on *Underground*, Kusturica still talked of *Crime and Punishment* as his major project from which he had simply taken some time off. *Underground* appeared to be a smaller project, a film he would make in-between, as a detour before returning to the emotionally engaging *Crime and Punishment*. In the course of work, however, things changed; the small *Underground* project became a titanic one while *Crime and Punishment* gradually faded out and eventually was dropped altogether. Kusturica abandoned the Dostoevsky adaptation as he realised that people today are no longer able to reflect deeply on the issue of murder. He would rather make a film entitled 'Why I Didn't Make Crime and Punishment' (Ciment, 1995, p. 24).

During the making of *Underground*, Kusturica also spoke of a script by an unnamed Serb author that he was interested in. It is the story of a Serbian man who is taken prisoner and falls in love with a young Muslim woman. Kusturica said he liked the story, but opted for *Underground* because that script did not include the important communist dimension. In interviews given in 2001 across Eastern Europe the director once again talked of a project to shoot a film revolving round a love story from the Bosnian War, saying that work on this project was imminent.

For a short while after *Underground* Kusturica was set to direct a comedy with Daniel Auteuil called *The King of Sweden on a Bicycle one Friday Afternoon*. These plans were dropped at the time when *Black Cat*, which was initially meant to be a short, turned into a full-length feature.

Two of the films that Kusturica did not make could have changed the director's profile substantially: *The Bridge on the Drina* (mid-1980s) and *The White Hotel* (late 1990s).

The Bridge on the Drina (1985–7)

After winning at Cannes in 1985, Kusturica came closer than ever to fulfilling his long-time dream of directing an adaptation of Ivo Andrić's *The Bridge on the Drina* (*Na Drini ćuprija*), the classic Bosnian novel of the Nobel Prize laureate. *New York Times* reporter Henry Kamm remarked that the prospect of filming the novel was 'the only topic that aroused the laconic director's enthusiasm during more than two hours of conversation', when they met in 1985. 'It will be very important, my biggest venture, the biggest film ever made in Yugoslavia,' Kusturica told Kamm excitedly, speaking of the novel as 'a bible of the people of the Balkans' (Kamm, 1985, p. 21). 'If the European politicians had read this book,' he said later, 'they wouldn't have made all the stupid misjudgments on my country' (Ciment 1995, p. 26).

On several occasions in the early 1990s, Kusturica also expressed interest in filming the other main novel of Andrić, *Days of the Consuls* (*Travnička hronika*).

It is not clear why Kusturica gave up the *Drina* project. According to his 1989 interview for *Positif*, he realised that there was no one to produce the film in the Serbian language, but, even if he could find a Western producer, he could not imagine having his Bosnian protagonists speak English. In the press kit for *Gypsies* he explains that 'the project was too big and I didn't dare undertake it'. In later interviews he indicates only that the film did not materialise because he did not think it possible to make this film in the English language. What remains unclear, however, is why he would need to make the film in English. Wasn't it possible to have foreign financing and still shoot in the local language? Wasn't his next film also financed internationally and shot in an even more obscure language, Romani? Was the Cannes-winning director prevented from working on the Andrić adaptation by the cultural administration at home? Did he think that the political climate in Yugoslavia at the time was unsuitable? I have not come across evidence to support any of these possible explanations. It seems more plausible that, after his Cannes success, Kusturica was looking for a project with international appeal, a context in which Andrić's historical epic appeared of narrow regional interest.

The decision not to make *The Bridge on the Drina* was a key one in Kusturica's career. Had he worked on the Andrić adaptation, he would have inevitably become a titan Balkan film-maker, deeply engaged with the region's historical predicament. From the moment he decided not to take this route, he began turning into the cosmopolitan post-modern auteur he is today.

The White Hotel (1998–2000)

For nearly two years, after *Black Cat*, Kusturica's name was linked to plans for adapting D. M. Thomas's 1981 novel *The White Hotel* from an existing script by the legendary British scriptwriter, the late Dennis Potter. It was to be produced by John Roberdeau and Michael Geisler and the financing was supposed to be from European and American sources. *Underground*'s Dušan Kovačević was brought in to adjust the script for Kusturica. He reportedly moved the action from Vienna to Berlin and substituted the old Freud with a young therapist with whom the protagonist falls in love (in the novel there is a substantial age difference between patient and psychoanalyst and their relationship is based on authority and guidance). Fellini's veteran cameraman Giuseppe Rotunno was enlisted as director of photography. The producers believed that the material was perfect for Kusturica because, as Geisler told *Daily Variety* 'Emir's movies can be so earthy and real, but they also have such a surrealistic spirit' (15 September, 1998, p. 5). Shooting was to take place across Europe: in the Italian Alps, Berlin and Montenegro. The film was to star Johnny Depp and David Thewlis, but it never became clear who would be cast in the female lead. A number of actresses of considerable box-office potential were mentioned, however (Nicole Kidman, Juliette Binoche, Kate Winslet, Cate Blanchett, Frances McDormand, Holly Hunter, Lena Olin, Irene Jacob). Plans for the film were dropped in 2000, after the producers ran into financial difficulties.

Had *The White Hotel* materialised, it could have pushed the director's career in a new direction. In the novel psychoanalysis and historical discourse intersect in a unique fashion. To Hayden White, it is a work in a new genre that combines the written and the visual in a post-modernist, parahistorical representation (White, 1997, p. 18). It problematises the limitations of psychoanalysis by confronting it with the ironies of history. Had Kusturica worked on this film, he would have had the chance to return to the topic of the Holocaust and to re-examine his approach to history. In addition, for the first time he would have worked with material centred on a complex female protagonist, a woman of great contradictions who struggles to balance a troubled sexuality with a high-profile career and distressed family and who ultimately perishes in the Holocaust. This project was a missed chance for Kusturica to show himself capable of a meaningful and wholesome treatment of such a female character.

The Nose (forthcoming?)

Most recently, Kusturica announced that he is committed to a project called *The Nose*, based on motifs from a Dušan Kovačević play. The producer on board is said to be Jean-François Fonlupt, formerly of CiBY 2000 and now of Emotion Pictures. It would be an English-language film set in New York, telling the story of a stage actor who is playing Cyrano de Bergerac and who has to rescue someone from the hands of Russian mobsters. As the Russian Mafia is promised to feature prominently in this film, it may mean a partial return to Dostoevskian themes, but it also seems to return to Gogol's grotesque tale of a detached nose that chases the protagonist. In interviews in 2001 Kusturica spoke of his interest in the psychology of the Russian Mafiosi whom he compared to Gypsies – living by simple laws and confessing simple values but nonetheless possessed by Shakespearean feelings in a tragic confrontation of intellect, ethics and emotion. Information available on the Internet Movie Database in 2001 informs us that this will be a film for those who liked Guy Ritchie's *Snatch* (2000) and the Coen brothers' *O, Brother, Where Art Thou?* (2000).

The next film

According to most recent reports, however, *The Nose* is also a project of the past, abandoned in favour of a film which is now in pre-production and will be shot in Yugoslavia in 2002. Under the working title *Hungry Heart*, the film is said to revolve around a love story from the time of the Bosnian War. The project will bring together those of Kusturica's traditional collaborators who are still devoted to him. The film will be internationally financed and will be part of a three-picture deal that the director has reportedly signed with the French StudioCanal.

Three
The Artistry

In Lyotard's definition, no pre-established rules govern the work of the post-modern artist and he cannot be judged within the familiar set of categories. New rules and new categories are created; post-modern art is no longer 'text' but 'event'. 'The emphasis can also be placed on the increase of being and the jubilation which results from the invention of new rules of the game, be it pictorial, artistic, or any other' (Lyotard, 1981, pp. 79–80).

This seems to fully apply in Kusturica's case. Even though his artistry can be dissected and analysed within traditional frameworks that look at aesthetics, *mise-en-scène* and narrative, he consistently defies prescribed procedures for the sake of an increased 'being and jubilation', and for the sake of exchanging energy with his audiences.

I do not think, however, that the work of a baroque film-maker should necessarily require baroque criticism. So I will approach Kusturica's work by using a set of more traditional critical methods. I will look into the elements that make up Kusturica's lavish cinematic style. I will discuss the director's *mise-en-scène*, image inventory and leading narrative tropes, as well as his recycling of particular artistic influences. I hope this will help to understand the controlled chaos that characterises Kusturica's artistic universe.

Aesthetics

Kusturica employs and simultaneously subverts traditional aesthetic categories. He plays with the beautiful and the ugly, the sublime and the despicable, the comic and the tragic. These oppositions supplement each other in a constantly changing interplay of mutual recreation.

The traditional set of aesthetic concepts does not really cover Kusturica's artistic universe. A different range of categories comes into play here: the flamboyant, the exuberant, the dreamlike, the subversive, the carnivalesque, the grotesque, the Dionysian, the sombre, the intense, the baroque, the spectacular and, most recognisably, the one of the magic realist.

Critics have paid explicit attention to the baroque feel of Kusturica's work, usually associated with excessive ornamentation, with overwhelming luxuriance, with an overabundance of little details that, when brought together, make for an overwhelming experience of splendour and profusion. His extravagantly ornate forms and exuberant decorations, however, do not result from some conscious interest in the baroque period in art (seventeenth–eighteenth century). It is much rather a post-modern interest in spontaneously combining incongruous elements into a convoluted abundance. Talking of *Gypsies*, Kusturica recalled seeing a photo of a Gypsy man returning to Yugoslavia from France: 'He was driving some kind of French car, a Peugeot maybe and on top of it was a 14th century table – I really think it was authentic – and some very modern chairs. He looked like a cowboy, with a 10-gallon hat and a plaid shirt' (Thomas, 1990, p. 6). Elsewhere, he described how he saw a Gypsy man who was wearing a fascinating combination of clothes, not only totally incompatible but also far too many:

> On top of his shirt he wears three T-shirts of different colours, his trousers look as if they have come from another planet. This is a film where everything is mixed together, simply because this is what life is like. Cinema pulled together video, television, music and literature, it cannot help but have this baroque form.

Kusturica, quoted in Katsahnias, 1989, p. 38

Kusturica's 'baroque' seems to originate from his interest in the Roma and it first emerges in the style of *Gypsies*. Since then it has become a defining element in his approach to cinema: bringing together a variety of details, making sure that the elements are not only discordant, but that there are plenty of little things that do not fit but nonetheless find a place in the picture. The protagonist of *Guernica* creates a collage of family photographs cut in pieces and in the later films there are overwhelming numbers of photographs on the walls. It is an approach reminiscent of Czechoslovak surrealists Jan Svankmajer and Juraj Jakubisko and of Buñuel's *Viridiana* (1961).

Another dimension of the baroque is kitsch, a category that Kusturica himself used when discussing *Arizona Dream*. He stated that he believed in the power of kitsch (Bouineau, 1993, p. 62), that he thinks of America as kitsch, symbolised by the pink house of Jerry Lewis (Ciment, 1993, p. 23) and that Russians and Americans are the champions of kitsch (Ciment, 1995, p. 27). His example of the Gypsy man with all the absurd layers of clothing suggests that it is precisely this excess and incompatibility that the director has made sure to recreate and supply with aesthetic value.

The spectacular is yet another non-traditional aesthetic category which seems particularly suited to an understanding of Kusturica's work. The first wedding scene in *Underground*, even though taking place in a cellar, is spectacular. The final wedding scene in *Underground* is even more so, and the feast that takes place in *Black Cat* is spectacular as well.

Traditionally used to describe the quality of landscape, in Kusturica the category of the spectacular more appropriately relates to the behaviour of certain protagonists, thus essentialising their spontaneity. Not nature but people are spectacular here: vital, exuberant and restless. The flamboyant Ahmed in *Gypsies*, Marko and Blacky in *Underground*, Dadan and Grga Pitić in *Black Cat*, with their superior energy and never-ending zeal to drink, dance and enjoy, are all spectacular.

Most frequently, Kusturica's cinema has been described as 'magic realist', a concept that is used to connote the fantastic and surrealist elements that the director has persistently traced back to the influence of Márquez. Speaking to the media about *Gypsies*, a film where rich folklore and fantastic events are woven into the film's fabric, Kusturica kept mentioning magic-realist fiction. 'I need a little more realism, but with an occasional surrealistic event bursting out of that realism' (press kit for *Gypsies*, 1989).

In addition to literature, Kusturica's 'magic realism' has been traced to the work of Chagall and to Yugoslav naïve painting, as well as Buñuel's surrealism. The majority of magic elements in *Gypsies*, however, can be traced most appropriately to Tarkovsky: telekinetic abilities, levitation, flight over water.

It is the surreal, conditional feeling of reality that Kusturica has made his signature approach to cinema and has been constant in all his work since

Gypsies. Even though some of the fantasy elements do not derive naturally from the narrative they are brought in as a trademark visual element. Magic elements are present (albeit not prevailing) in *Arizona* – the flying fish, the ambulance and the dream of the extreme North. They are also found in *Underground* – the flying bride, the underwater encounters with loved ones and the final celebration on the shore. Fairy-tale references are scattered throughout *Black Cat*. But it is *Gypsies* that remains the ultimate magic realist film of the director. It is only in this film that things happening in a dream (Perhan and Azra's sexual initiation on St George's Day) have an impact on their lives later on, with Azra's miraculous pregnancy reminiscent of an immaculate conception, a fantasy that Christians have been fascinated with for centuries.

In order to distinguish his own views on fantasy aesthetics, Kusturica has frequently spoken out against what he calls 'naturalism'. Even though he has not exactly defined the concept, 'naturalism' in his usage describes the TV-minded production values of Hollywood that are being aggressively imposed on the movies nowadays.

Poetics

> The most important thing is to use the camera to establish a link to the spectator, to make your subjective vision connect things and people [...] I prefer a 'punk' way to use the camera, a mixture of beauty and rubbish and most of all to establish links between all the elements of the surface (plateau).
>
> Kusturica, quoted in Ciment, 1995, p. 28

In working on the *mise-en-scène*, Kusturica is a perfectionist. He thinks of all the elements that come together within the frame in each sequence. What he seeks to achieve, however, is not a stylish and sleek look. He prefers the dishevelled to the groomed and the disorderly to the trimmed, thus creating the unique curvatious feel of his films. He likes to create a complex reality crammed with scores of gadgets, extras, ornaments and many other little things. He then lets the protagonists make their way through it all. And then he records their manoeuvres on film by using a camera which, while filming, rotates or moves up and down, forward and backward and sideways. The director's role is to 'coordinate and balance the energy' (press kit for *Gypsies*, 1989), governing 'the way energy and feelings are transposed onto the screen', an experience similar to 'weaving rugs' (Bouineau, 1993, pp. 46 and 49).

Layers of occurrences

> The problem in the type of films that I make is to maintain a fruitful relationship between the background, with all its complex signification and the foreground where I use the means I have at my disposal to keep the spectator elevated.
>
> Kusturica, quoted in Ciment, 1995, p. 22

Kusturica talks of the equal importance of background, midground and foreground and of his explicit attention to making the midground and the background particularly vivid. He talks of his *mise-en-scène* as a moving mosaic and notes that it is difficult for him to distinguish the central thing that is happening in a scene because he does not approach it as rationally and logically as other film-makers. It is all equally important, to the last detail, and it is all moving and evolving at every moment.

The multiple layers of occurrences in Kusturica's pictorial language become increasingly complex with time, and currently we can talk of Kusturica's style as one that combines such layers within each sequence and frame. This elaborate choreography involves complex *mise-en-scènes*, where the whole seems on the brink of collapsing, but is miraculously kept under control by the director who brings it all together and balances the entropy.

One of the best illustrations of Kusturica's multi-layered *mise-en-scène* is found early on, in *Father*. The setting is the wedding in the courtyard at the end of the film. Viewers have been exposed to the family's adulteries, betrayals and adversities for the past two hours. At this critical moment all the family members are together again, seated at the same table, drunk and remorseful to the accompaniment of endless songs. Old antagonisms are temporarily suppressed, but only on the surface, as new passions arise and are played out. People are seen coming and going around the π-shaped table. In the background, while playing with his new football, Malik's attention is taken by something he sees through the basement window. We, the viewers, know what he sees – his father engaged in violent sex with Ankica, the aunt. In the general context of the scene, Malik's witnessing of this key event evolves only in a remote corner of the screen, while guests interacting with each other around the table take up the foreground. The viewer's knowledge of what Malik sees, however, changes the semantic space of the scene and endows the background with greater importance than the foreground. Thus, the multi-layered structure of the scene overthrows the common narrative logic of a traditional *mise-en-scène*.

This treatment of the layers of occurrences at a communal event becomes particularly important in Kusturica's later work. Several memorably choreographed scenes of this type are seen in *Gypsies*. In one of the opening sequences, for example, the camera pans extensively to show, within a single take, a variety of layered events: the uncle gambling in midground, then coming to the foreground to a water tap and praying to God for better luck, while in the background a boy buys bread, a wedding passes by with a cursing bride and a blind-drunk groom and so too do cows and vehicles.

A remarkable multi-layered sequence is that of Ahmed's assassination. The scene takes place in a large tent, amid a wedding crowd. The camera's complex movements are combined with a complex choreography of the moves of people and objects – Perhan, Irfan, Ahmed's brother, Ahmed, the bride, as well as a crowd of dancing guests, a flying fork and a white cake. This single-take scene lasts 2:07 minutes, during which the camera follows a number of events that evolve on all levels. It makes five sweeping movements:

1. Camera moving left–right: In the foreground we see Irfan making a sign to Perhan who is outside to come in.
2. Right–left: The camera turns to the right and then moves right–left, showing Perhan in midground coming in, passing through the crowd, being apprehended by one of Ahmed's brothers, taken to Ahmed and the bride, bowing in front of Ahmed, swearing allegiance and begging forgiveness.

3. Left–right: After he is granted forgiveness, Perhan is taken to the opposite end of the long table and seated. Here he concentrates his gaze onto the fork in front of him.

4. Right–left: The fork levitates and accelerates flying through the air, stabbing Ahmed in the neck, Ahmed falls dead, the crowd is overtaken by panic.

5. Left–right: the camera's gaze is diverted immediately back to the crowd to show Perhan in midground, now fighting with Ahmed's brother and overpowering him by pressing his face into a white wedding cake on the table and then escaping through the door.

For this scene, calculated and worked out with a high level of precision, Kusturica held the camera himself. The flying fork has been held by invisible threads and moved by a puppeteer hidden behind the wedding table. But the most important part is the special angle of shooting that allows for the *trompe l'oeil*. Hidden under his collar and concealed by make-up, a little blade has been attached to Ahmed's neck to kill the fork's speed and make sure that the splash of blood comes out at the right moment. It is not noticeable because of the speed of the shot and because the camera's eye turns back to Perhan almost immediately, as if to provide a continuation of the narrative but in fact to distract the viewer's attention.

It all happens to the accompaniment of continuous dancing and drinking; thus the assassination appears as only one of the multiple layers of occurrences here. Such a set-up strengthens the feeling of relativity – everything changes all the time, nothing stays the same and what may be the climax of one story evolves on the periphery of another. The Greek philosopher Heraclitus insisted we could never enter the same river twice, as it changes incessantly. Similarly, Kusturica's films keep changing, as new layers of occurrences come into focus at every viewing. We are constantly reminded of the conventionality of meaning, significance and signification.

In these complex scenes Kusturica divides his attention between at least three tiers and sometimes more. Take the cellar wedding in *Underground*. Foreground and background alternate as children with sparklers run around, engaged in the chase, living their own sequence of

events. Gypsy musicians play on a rotating platform, guests pass by; a fat
woman, a tank and a monkey are present. The protagonists are seated at a
table in middle ground, carrying the burden of intricate relationships
known to the viewer. The advent of the flying bride supplies an additional
dimension to the multi-layered structure of the scene. Delivered on a
special device, she arrives on top of the groom, touches down with a kiss
and takes her place at the table.

This multi-dimensionally scattered eventfulness is now enthroned as
the leading feature in Kusturica's *mise-en-scène*. It is so prevalent in *Black
Cat* that it comes across as an end in itself. Here, the pulsating layers supply
more vigour and dynamics than the intertwining plotlines, making the concept of narrative void of meaning.

In his staging of multiple layers of occurrences, Kusturica is comparable
to other directors who use similarly complex choreography, like Jancsó or
Angelopoulos. But his arrangements are fuzzier, moving more in curves and
frivolously changing direction, while theirs are more geometrical. In this,
Kusturica is closer to Fellini who does not plan as precisely but who brings
in the feel of incessant rhythm and dynamics.

The concept of 'musicality' is yet another way to refer to the important
coordination of layers of occurrence: apart from his interest in music,
Kusturica has spoken extensively about the 'musicality' of his films. Also
mentioned by cameraman Vilko Filač, Kusturica's most enduring collaborator, the concept is used to describe the way all different elements of the
film are brought together, creating a harmony that seems born out of disso-
nance. As with the Balkan and Romani folk songs he prefers to use, which
are characterised by their uneven rhythms, the musicality of Kusturica's
films also relies on an uneven and yet masterfully balanced arrangement of
images, movements and colours.

Everything about montage he learned from Fellini, Kusturica said, whose
movies he watched repeatedly while studying in Prague. It was here that he
understood how the dynamism of earlier scenes sustains the dynamics
needed for the later ones. Other lessons from Fellini were the use of parallel
montage and the combining of epic and dramatic structures. When editing,
Kusturica would normally start by putting together a four-hour-long version

of the film, which he would then gradually cut down to the final length, with the active help of the editor, 'who would put a new view on the film' (Bouineau, p. 88).

Rather than rely on post-production, the director would edit through his *mise-en-scène* and would repeat takes as many times as needed to get all the emotions and details right. The actual editing takes place during shooting, because only at this stage can emotions be portrayed elegantly.

On other occasions, however, Kusturica has indicated that editing is particularly important to him, especially when he is pursuing the development of several narratives at a time (Ciment, 1993, p. 24). Until all the little details come together at this stage, the film exists only in his imagination. He admitted that it was only during editing, for example, that he discovered and appreciated the visual potential of the spectacular river scene in *Gypsies* (Bouineau, 1993, p. 14).

Kusturica is famous for making his films too long for the traditional ninety-minute standard. Only *Dolly Bell* runs under two hours. All the others are longer and many of them have had to be shortened from the intended directorial cut to attain the length of their eventual release. The potential for overlength is already present in the complex scripts that Kusturica prefers, with multiple intersecting subplots, all stories that simply cannot be told in brief. This choice of narratives, however, has compelled him to edit out plotlines and twists, often resulting in narrative incoherence.

Camera work

Jonathan Romney wrote: 'It is never simply a question of several things happening at once – ice blocks tumbling downstairs, while a bystander juggles with grenades – but of things happening in different directions' (1999).

The directions in Kusturica's *mise-en-scène*, however, are not as numerous as it seems. Diagonal moves do not really happen and the camera rarely ventures into the depth of the scene (the feeling of depth comes from the superimposed multiple layers).

Kusturica constructs his scenes around the vertical and horizontal axes, an opposition which, he admits, 'is present in each one of my works'

(Beauchamp and Grugeau, 1990, p. 57). He also uses a lot of rotations and revolving camera movements.

In a typical Kusturica scene the important moves of the characters are made vertically. These entrances and exits are most articulate in *Underground*, where the protagonists come and go through vertical openings all the time: Marko and Blacky descend into tunnels, Marko appears from under the floor of the hospital where Blacky is detained, the bride jumps down in a well, Ivan climbs up through a vertical opening to resurface from the tunnel network below Europe, and so on.

The scenes that involve a crowd are usually constructed horizontally and rely on a tracking camera movement that follows the moves of the protagonists across the screen (best seen in the flying fork sequence in *Gypsies*). Such scenes usually include several horizontal moves of the camera back and forth within a single take. It is often the case that while the camera moves horizontally in one direction, say from left to right, the protagonists are asked to move in the opposite direction, from right to left, thus giving the scene a more vibrant feel. This seems to be a Fellini influence: his horizontally set sequences feature camera and people moving in opposite directions. A typical shot in *Amarcord*, for example, is of the town's promenade, where strolling people pass each other, a fairly flat two-dimensional scene that is given a multi-layered feel by the disturbances coming from the movement of running boys and a young woman in disarray.

Besides the horizontal tracking, the camera particularly favours rotation and circular movement. As early as *Brides* Kusturica and Filač construct a scene where the camera rotates at 360 degrees, tracking the attempts of Martin to break into the circle of men gathered around his 'bride', while she remains out of sight in the middle (which is also the camera's point of view). In *Arizona* the camera circles around the table on several occasions, most notably during Elaine's dinner party and the Russian roulette scene.

Rotational camera movements abound in *Underground*, enhanced by the use of round objects (e.g. table, well) and rotating platforms for the cameraman. Pavle Levi has appropriately noted that the two most notable gyrate formations of this sort are:

(a) the extreme low-angle medium-close shot which depicts Marko, Blacky and Natalija singing directly into the camera, as their interlocking bodies begin to spin around the axis extending from the camera to the characters' plane of action and

(b) the actual spinning-wheel, built by the inhabitants of the underground, kept in their cellar and used for festivities and celebrations. The Romani musicians play standing on the wheel, which spins ever more faster until their bodies turn into a visual blur.

'What is common to these two rotating patterns,' Levi writes, 'is that they both generate a strong impression of an efferent force at work – a force that tends to pull the exuberant enjoyment away from its corporeal "containers", into an expanded (social) field' (2001, p. 13).

The position of the camera is of particular importance and many clever devices assist the director of photography in his work on complex shots. Camera assistants, dollies, cranes, platforms and rails are used to secure the camera movements that travel up and down, from side to side and in panning shots. As far as special effects are concerned, they are neither too many nor too costly. Without them, however, his films simply would not be what they are. Whenever he has used magic elements – a flying veil, fork or fish, or scenes of levitation or telekinesis – they have left a lasting impression. 'The big American productions use special effects for entertainment purposes. I think that the tricks have a different function: a more poetic, more organic one', the director told Ciment and Codelli (1989, p. 8). Overall, illusion is deployed sparingly and it is the masterful usage of accentuated fantasy elements that gives the magic feel. The economic handling of a few carefully positioned dreamlike elements has a strong enchanting effect, as it requires the spectator's imagination to work intensely.

More of the fantasy elements are achieved through careful planning of long and complex takes and with the use of clever devices, and only a few with montage. In *Time of the Gypsies*, for example, the only lab-made special effect was the angel-like appearance of the turkey's soul in the sky at the time of Perhan's death. In *Underground* the use of digital technology was limited to the grafting of the protagonists into sequences of archival footage. All the other effects were achieved with 'bric-a-brac' and made the director feel like a 'charlatan', as he told Katsahnias in 1989. In most cases it comes down to smartly constructed devices that are in the frame but are cleverly made invisible to the viewer, whether by the camera angle, the colour combination, or elements in the *mise-en-scène*. The scene of Perhan's dream, for example, when he descends over the river holding his turkey, was shot by using a forty metre-tall crane where Perhan was placed on one platform and the camera on another.

Intensity

Kusturica's early films are typical East European fare: edited at a relatively slow pace and offering a moderately timed narrative. The issue of pacing, it seems, only comes to concern the director after the success of *Father*. He does not immediately resort to faster pacing, but he changes the tempo of his narration. Even though in *Gypsies* he experiments with some Tarkovsky-Jancsó-style complexly choreographed sequences, he creates them differently, by using a more dynamic camera and faster action, by staging a more intense show for the camera and getting an increased level of intensity in every subsequent scene. The complexity of sequences remains somehow inconspicuous, evading parallels to the contemplative feel of Tarkovsky and Jancsó's constructed scenes. No intentional stylisation is felt here due to the dynamic motion and the multiple layers of happenings that make Kusturica's tableaux vibrant and eventful rather than static or solemn.

With time, the issues of pacing become of increasing importance. 'I am doing with the tempo something that I learned from the American cinema,' the director said to Feinstein. 'It's like a movie that starts like a hurricane and finishes like another type of storm' (1999, p.2/7).

After the release of *Arizona* Kusturica underlined that he worked a lot on the film's pacing. And indeed, it seems that the shots here are of shorter duration and the cutting more dynamic. But this newly acquired dynamism is compromised by an overburdened plotline, also evident in *Underground* and *Black Cat*. Even though the formal pacing of the film is accelerated, the cutting is frequent and the rhythm is enhanced by music and dancing on screen, these films leave the impression of an over-lengthy show. It is not a problem of editing or *mise-en-scène*, but of the director's indulgence in convoluted narratives.

Light, colour and sound

Balancing light, colour and sound in a seemingly dissonant and yet harmonious whole is the key to the vibrant multiplicity of layers. Kusturica prefers low-key lighting and darker colours, particularly seen in early films like *Bar Titanic* and *Dolly Bell*, but also later on in *Underground*. Seemingly influenced by Welles and Tarkovsky, he develops a taste for highlighting articulate shadows that the protagonists cast on the walls. High-key lighting is mostly used to contrast some scenes from the predominant low-key mode, as seen in the wedding at the end of *Underground*.

While shooting *Underground* in Prague, Kusturica continually complained that the light was not right and he left many of the outdoor Belgrade scenes to be shot later on location. Natural light was of particular importance also in *Black Cat*, a film that was shot strictly between eleven in the morning and three in the afternoon. Due to persistent bad weather during the first summer on the set, the shooting was cancelled and the completion of the film was postponed for a year in order to ensure a consistent quality of light.

In Kusturica's films colour is approached in nearly pointillist manner. In almost every important frame there is a small but intensely coloured red spot that balances the rest of the picture even when located outside the actual centre of the action. The red comes from some natural element that just seems to be there accidentally – a vase with a red flower, a bouquet of red roses or carnations, a lamp, a pillow, a singer's dress, a flag, a pioneer tie, a red box on a shelf, a red balloon, or sugar coated red apples. Extensively exploited in cinema – from *The Wizard of Oz* (V. Fleming, 1939) and *The Red Shoes* (Powell and Pressburger, 1948) to Tati's *Playtime* (1967), Fellini's *Amarcord* and Schlöndorff's *Blechtrommel* (*The Tin Drum*, 1979) – the visual quality of the red spot is an enduring element in Kusturica's aesthetics. It appears as early as *Titanic*, becomes a permanent presence around the time of *Father* and has not disappeared from the director's work since, claiming a prominent pace in *Gypsies* and thereafter.

Not as conspicuous as the red, the white spot blends more naturally with the natural colours of the environment. It is present throughout Kusturica's films, occasionally even prevailing: white flags, scarves and flowers. When asked about the frequent use of a flock of geese in his Romani films, for example, Kusturica explains it as a needed colour spot.

Although not as persistent as the white and the red, other colour spots are also present in *Father* and in *Gypsies*. Occasional green spots (watermelons, a motorcycle) are used in *Underground*. In *Black Cat* the spots grow even more diverse. There is still the white/red combination (e.g. the ice cream that Zare brings to Ida), but numerous other intense colour spots are added: blue, yellow, pink, green and brownish orange, all reminiscent of an early image of a colourful parasol seen in *Brides*.

Sound in Kusturica is used in symbiosis with colour and light, most often to complement or enhance the aesthetic effect of pacing and to add extra dimensions to the multiple layers of occurrence. Sound is more often diegetic than not: if music is heard, it is made by someone who is also seen on screen – a person singing, playing the accordion, the guitar, or the tambura, or a Romani brass band, an important stylistic device directly accounting for an elevated and agitated atmosphere.

But Kusturica has used sound in a variety of ways. Dramatic choir arrangements are heard in the background of each dramatic event in *Gypsies* and *Arizona*. In *Father* the director extensively deploys soundtrack of radio voices, most notably of football broadcasts. The scene in which the father gets the crucial phone call that summons him to security headquarters is played out entirely against the soundtrack of a heated commentary of a football match. What the spectators hear is the radio voice; what they see is the face of the father, sobering up at the call. Here, sound juxtaposes the image.

Such juxtaposition, reminiscent of Makavejev's use of music, is also used in a more intricate (and politically saturated) line of signification – the revolutionary *Warszawjanka* is sung in *Dolly Bell* and the Nazi song *Lili Marleen* is played to footage of Tito's funeral in *Underground*.

From early on, Kusturica was privileged to work with one of the best-known Yugoslav film composers, Zoran Simjanović (b. 1946), who was responsible for the music to his *Dolly Bell* and *Father* and who had worked closely with the other directors of the Prague group. For *Gypsies*, he was paired with the Sarajevan celebrity Goran Bregović (b. 1950), at the time a leader of the rock group Bjelo Dugme (White Button), one of the most popular rock formations in Yugoslavia. An idiosyncratic musical talent, Bregović is a post-modern 'fusion' musician whose work consists in collating and adapting folklore melodies from around the world to contemporary rhythms. Even though in the late 1990s the two of them split, in the press kit for *Underground* Kusturica stressed that he and Bregović 'have the same roots and share a very harmonious relationship'. All the music Bregović created for Kusturica has become extremely popular and in certain regions of Eastern Europe he rivals and sometimes surpasses Kusturica in popularity. The Romani songs from *Gypsies* and in particular his treatment of *Ederlezi* (St George's Day song), have become something like national anthems, sung at weddings and various other celebrations across Yugoslavia. The music for *Underground* is an essential element of the frantic rhythm of the film and was often performed on set, simultaneously with the shooting.

Narrative

The narrative is supposed to enhance the rich texture of the *mise-en-scène*; the events of the story are to supply an extra dimension to the layers of occurrences and fill them with energy and exuberance, being and jubilation.

It was Gabriel García Márquez, Kusturica said, who radically shaped his views on storytelling and from whom he 'learned the freedom to blend the narrative in circles' (Feinstein, 1996, p. 78). Today, the typical Kusturica film is one where multiple subplots intermingle in a fragile narrative that can disintegrate at almost any time. It is impossible for the spectator to predict what will happen next, making the viewing a profoundly engaging experience. In addition, Kusturica said he preferred to end his stories 'with an open door', on a calm note, 'like after a violent and passionate love act' (Bouineau, 1993, pp. 68 and 67).

But it did not start off like this. The preference for loosely constructed narratives that border on chaos and can change direction at any moment developed gradually over time. In his early films Kusturica was still inclined to use straightforward narratives which he would adjust to his aesthetic views. This resulted in a 'mosaic' approach, one that mainly relied on telling the story by keeping a subtle tension between what is known to the protagonists in the film and what is known to the viewers in the theatre, with the 'final pattern understood only by the viewer' (Horton, 1988, p. 72). Even when the narrator was clearly identified (Malik in *Father*, Axel in *Arizona*) Kusturica maintained the interplay of overt and covert narrative and told the story from alternating points of view. In his detailed analysis of *Father*, for example, Horton showed that even though on the surface the story is told from Malik's point of view, in fact there are multiple narrative voices. Kusturica's weaving of overt and covert discourse, Horton wrote, worked 'against the sense of continuity and redundancy that characterize classical American cinema', and positioned his films as 'a *contrast* to classical cinema rather than a radical destruction of such a paradigm' (1988, p. 74). It was more or less the same with Axel, the protagonist of *Arizona* – this was supposedly a first-person narrative, but not all the events were told from Axel's point of view and he could not have witnessed some key episodes.

Back in the mid-1980s, Kusturica seemed bound to become a director of films tackling collisions between the individual and history. But after parting with screenwriter Abdulah Sidran and giving up the *Drina* project, he took a different direction, rapidly moving away from the epic form that, until then, he seemed to have been approaching. Even though Kusturica's interest in post-modern epic narratives appeared reinvigorated in the 1990s (with *Underground* and his commitment to directing *The White Hotel*), from where we stand in the present it does not seem to have been a lasting revival.

Even though he speaks of melodrama as one of his favourite genres (Ciment, 1993, p. 22) and classifies the films of Fassbinder and Wenders as its best examples (Bertellini 1995, p. 38), Kusturica cannot be said to work in a particular genre. He is far removed from the idea of adherence to prescriptive canons. His subversive attitude to genre is noticeable even in his earliest work, when he is careful to include elements in the script that defy genre categorisation. Serious films, he said, cannot fit any single genre:

> A serious movie, like a serious novel, should comprise all fundamental, existential characteristics of human life: birth, growing up, grandmother, father, mother, it ought to consider at least in passing all those existential moments situated between birth and death and once it does that, it ceases to be a genre.
>
> Press kit for *Time of the Gypsies*

In *Arizona*, for example, Kusturica constantly defies all expectations of the development of a plotline according to traditional genre conventions. This is done by using casting against type (Jerry Lewis) and by blending romantic comedy, drama, thriller, action, *film noir*, Western and family saga. The film contains elements of all these, but only to subvert them. The fact that the genre of *Arizona* is impossible to define may be partially accountable for the film's failure to please Americans, but it may be also the reason for some critics' fascination with the film.

Some of Kusturica's films can be placed in the category of drama or history, but neither one of these strictly applies. The only specific feature that applies to Kusturica genre-wise is the coming-of-age story: many of his works trace the gradual transition from simple-hearted adolescence to corrupt maturity. These coming-of-age narratives are strictly linear and keep to a chronology of events, even if making abrupt jumps in time. Flashbacks are not used and backgrounds to the protagonists are rarely supplied. (The only two exceptions are in *Titanic* and in *Arizona* where Axel's past is introduced in the form of a home movie.) He concentrates on individual experiences, and believes that every film should comprise several important elements: love, death, birth (Bouineau, p. 45). No wonder then that *Father* is subtitled a 'historical love film', and *Gypsies*, 'a love film'.

Kusturica's typical protagonist is a male teenager or else an immature soul, often coming across as a misfit. He is of an ordinary background, usually on the lower end of what can be described as middle class. In the earlier films there is a clearly defined central figure whose experiences and feelings the viewers are expected to share to some extent (Dino, Malik, Perhan,

even Axel). Since *Underground*, however, identification with the protagonists is no longer presupposed or even expected. The characters are to be
observed, loathed or admired, but there is no protagonist whose motives
and feelings are to be empathised and sympathised with.

Like Sergio Leone and Fellini, Kusturica relies strongly on actors who
bring to the film impressive faces and an exciting presence. The cast in his
films is a combination of two types of acting talent – reputable professional
actors on the one hand and, on the other, amateurs who he has discovered
himself or with the assistance of friends and co-workers. An amateur who
fascinated Kusturica by having a face that could transform from ugly to
beautiful was the late Davor Dujmović (1969–1999), who was discovered by
the director in Sarajevo at the age of thirteen and appeared in several of his
films, most notably as Perhan in *Gypsies*.

For all his reputation for magic realism, Kusturica does not use the carefully designed non-linear narrative quirks that are a basic device used by
others in creating a magic feel. He relies on other devices of a more spatial
and visual nature, paying special attention to categories of locale: above and
below, in and out.

Dichotomies of locale

Kusturica often constructs his scenes in a way that allows the viewer to per-
ceive two different levels of a story – the one that evolves above (appearance) and the one that remains below (essence). Typical examples are the
numerous scenes that take place around a table. On top we see people sitting
and talking, but as soon as the camera moves underneath, a different picture
of intense erotic labours emerges, involving stretched legs and hands. On
one occasion a child (Malik) even sets those on top on fire. The division is
employed in *Father*, *Arizona* and *Underground*. In *Black Cat*, while the wedding is being celebrated on top, the bride runs away under the table, thus
effectively undermining the justification for the celebration on the upper
level. 'This opposition is effectively very cinematographic,' the director tells
Jousse and Grünberg (1995, p. 69).

The above and below dichotomy is the backbone of numerous scenes
that are structured around a protagonist overlooking some event that

evolves below from a higher window. Being above, behind the window, means being cut off and unable to intervene (Dino watches Dolly Bell being taken away on Pog's motorbike, Axel sees the suicidal Grace walking in the rain carrying a pistol).

In *Underground* the above/below dichotomy is made the basis of the narrative. Here the juxtaposition does not translate into essence and appearance, as everything proves elusive; it is about an endless cycle of sinking downwards. Still, the underground system of tunnels, facilitating lively exchanges at the height of the Cold War while strict divisions are imposed on top, suggests the same juxtaposition of action below countering stagnation on the surface.

Then, there is the dichotomy of indoors and outdoors. Although this usually translates into a dichotomy of private and public space, this is not the case in Kusturica. A key episode in *Gypsies* – the lifting of Perhan's house

What moments earlier was a shelter, a private space where Perhan's family could sleep safely, turns, in a matter of seconds, into an open stage where they are exposed to rain and ridicule (*Time of the Gypsies*, 1989)

by crane — summarises the interplay of these categories. What moments earlier was a shelter, a private space where Perhan's family could sleep safely turns, in a matter of seconds, into an open stage where they endure rain and ridicule. They are all wet under the cardboard house hanging in the air, exposed to an apocalyptic thunderstorm at the whim of the uncle gone mad. Everything breaks apart, rain pours over the precious family photographs. It is a surreal picture of devastation, of a distressful deprivation of privacy. Perhan will never regain a private space: his next 'home', a place to sleep in Italy, will be in an abandoned school bus.

The setting in which Kusturica's protagonists feel best is a fragile space that is not fortified and may even be in the open air, and yet is somehow part sheltered and private, accessible only to a select few, like the joyous outdoors inhabited by the protagonists of *Black Cat*. It is a space located near the house ('home') but different from it — Dino's pigeonhouse, Malik's courtyard, Perhan's limestone oven and Elaine's porch. And similarly, the chunk of land with the wedding table in *Underground*, a happy open air but self-contained space that receives its meaning from the concept of 'home'.

It is the bed rather than the house that is really homey in *Brides, Dolly Bell, Father* and *Gypsies*. Other recurrent images speak of the need for some small private, cosy and sheltering space, from where 'you can see everyone but no one can see you,' as Axel notes in *Arizona Dream*. Such spaces, for example, are the mobile cardboard boxes driven by invisible kids hidden inside, with holes for the eyes. They first appear in *Gypsies*, but are also present in *Black Cat*, where Afrodita, the reluctant bride, uses one to escape from the wedding. The image is also replicated in a moving hollow tree trunk under which Afrodita hides during her run. Further variations of the cosy private shelter are the recurrent images of outhouse cubicles, from where the world can be observed through a heart-shaped hole on the door, or the image of a young man hiding under the skirts of a woman (Axel under Elaine's lace skirts, Zare under Ida's).

Even though the director has spoken of the use of various elements of nature (e.g. sky, desert and trees), nature does not have a prominent place in Kusturica's films and no particular type of landscape or natural image is

The cardboard boxes that move around driven by invisible kids hidden inside are little private, cosy and sheltering spaces, from where 'you can see everyone but no one can see you' (*Time of the Gypsies*)

a hallmark of his cinema. As in Vigo's *L'Atalante* and de Sica's *Miracolo a Milano* (*Miracle in Milan*, 1951), where the protagonists inhabit some peripheral space adjacent to city life, Kusturica's real locales are the urban margins. In narrative terms, these locales are self-contained and do not imply a centrifugal movement that unites them around a conditionally postulated centre.

This, inevitably, determines the moves that his protagonists undertake – from one periphery to another, from one marginal status to another. They are not troubled by the idea that they may spend their lives moving from one peripheral location to another, ignoring an imagined hierarchy of locations. Dino, who lives in the confining outskirts of the city, dreams of a move to the apartment complex, the new spaces of communist confinement in the housing projects. In *Gypsies*, Perhan moves from Šutka, the Skopje ghetto on the margins of Yugoslavia, to a makeshift settlement on the roadside in

Lombardy. Even though we see him moving around the very centre of Milan, near the cathedral and the Corso Vittorio Emanuele, he lives in the trailer camp near the suburban highway.

Kusturica prefers scattered architectural environments that are not organised around a specified centrepiece. His Sarajevo films do not contain a single glimpse of an architectural landmark: all the action takes place in narrow dwellings, courtyards, steep cobblestoned streets and a pigeonhouse. The characters in *Gypsies* inhabit one-room cardboard houses or trailers, the Eskimos in *Arizona* live in an igloo and Axel sleeps on the back of a truck in New York. The houses of Leo Sweetie and Elaine epitomise two different kinds of equally bad taste. Similarly tasteless are Marko's excessively ornate

In Perhan's second dream, Hatidža is displaced from the ghetto to the piazza of the Milan Cathedral (*Time of the Gypsies*)

house in *Underground* and the lavish and exotic interiors of Dadan's and Grga Pitić's mansions in *Black Cat*.

The director thought the architecture of Prague imposing; it depressed him while living there. The grandiose architecture of cities like Milan and Rome – majestic cathedrals, generous fountains and wide boulevards – is filmed in a way that suggests a similar degree of alienation. The protagonists of *Gypsies* are much more at home in the Fellinesque open spaces punctuated by scaffolds and billboards and in the tent camp amidst ancient Roman ruins in the outskirts of Rome.

Even though using architectural elements reminiscent of Tarkovsky (ruins, rail tracks, remote houses) and Fellini (city outskirts, scaffolds and roomy but confining interiors), Kusturica's use of architecture is profoundly different. Architectural connotations are most often used as a background onto which the protagonists project feelings and desires. In *Dolly Bell*, for example, the neon signs of hotels and the flashing image of a high-rise suggest a longing for something unspecified but resolutely modern. Cities are regularly shot from afar, more often as unattainable location than as friendly habitat. The elaborate architecture of the cellar and the tunnels in *Underground* are confusing environments, where the traditional concepts of location and destination, above and below, East and West, North and South, as well as their respective hierarchical cultural connotations, are subverted.

Oneirism

My imagination has been shaped by a world where the systems of communication are less rigid and much more metaphorical than in the rationalist and Cartesian countries.

Kusturica, quoted in Elhem, 1993, p.20

Dreams and oneiric references make an important part of this metaphorical communication, a sphere where the influence of Vigo, Buñuel and Tarkovsky is significant.

The preoccupation of *Dolly Bell*'s Dino with hypnosis (he also says he dreams of flying) and *Father*'s Malik with sleepwalking give an early indication of Kusturica's interest in oneirism. But it is not until *Gypsies* that dream sequences are actually introduced. The film contains two extended dreams that Perhan has, the first one of which, the St George's Day celebration on the river and his sexual initiation, is the film's highlight. The second, in which Perhan dreams of home during his Italian ordeal, is less impressive but equally important for the plot and represents Perhan's passage into maturity. Gimmicks and 'tricks' were used to create some powerful images, like the flying veil that symbolises the dead mother watching over her children when they are taken away. Just before her death, Azra levitates à la Tarkovsky, the levitation actually staged by lifting the actress on a device that is rendered invisible by the smart positioning of the camera and the inclusion of rail tracks and a passing train on the background.

According to Bertellini (1996, p. 70) the function of dreams, hypnosis or sleepwalking in the earlier films has been to oppose an overbearing public dimension and to help cultivate a personal space. In contrast, in *Gypsies* public and private are blurred and the dream is specifically positioned as an intermediary space which includes elements like water and fire, sky and earth, sun and moon, all mentioned in the Romani legend that is introduced earlier in the film. This cinematic translation of cosmogony is meant to pay a special tribute to Romani mythology and culture.

Gypsies also has a number of scenes that are not dreams but have a dreamlike feel – the veil that follows the Gypsy children as a guardian angel, Azra's levitation and the white flying turkey representing Perhan's soul at his death. The same combination of dreams and magic elements involving flying objects is seen in *Arizona*, particularly the flying fish symbolising Axel's loneliness and insecurity. To Kusturica, it stands for 'something huge, immense, a kind of opposition against a rational explanation of humanity's history' (Bouineau, 1993, p. 54).

The dreamlike effects in *Underground*, once again the result of clever devices constructed by production designer and genius of gimmicks Kreka, are exclusively related to the cellar wedding. The subsequent underwater encounters generate a poetic feel linked to the young couple Jovan and Jelena and their unrealised love. *Black Cat* could easily include dreams or dreamlike sequences, but it does not, maybe because they would overburden the already excessively convoluted plot. But the main reason for the gradual reduction and disappearance of dreams and magic elements from Kusturica's later work is, in my view, the absence of a clear-cut protagonist with whom the viewer could identify even conditionally, one whose dreams could be understood and empathised with.

Wedding

The wedding, a key narrative trope in Kusturica, has become a compulsory element since the time of *Father*. The director is known for altering scripts to make sure a wedding appears in each film, thus subjugating the narrative to his fondness for a certain visual element. 'This is undoubtedly an obsession,' he tells Ciment (1998, p. 22). Since *Gypsies* folklore and fantasy blend in the hallucinatory image of the floating bride, also seen in the heavy air of the confined space and in the underwater scene in *Underground*.

Weddings are centrepieces of Balkan films and Kusturica's are no exception to the rule. Here, multiple layers of interpersonal discomfort, gender inequality and controversial social dynamics taint the festive spirit on the surface. Cheerful dancing and elaborate rituals only enhance the underlying tensions. Conflict inevitably erupts as passions heat up after a few drinks and one cannot even say it happens unexpectedly; it is rather regarded as part of the normal course of events. All animosities and jealousies become visible, almost palpable at the wedding.

In Kusturica, the wedding is a metaphor for coming of age, while marriage is equated with maturity. The wedding is a rite of passage to the gloom of maturity and, as far the narrative is concerned, the wedding functions as a site of rupture. Where there is a wedding, the 'happily ever after' of married life that follows is left out of the narrative. The wedding is either set at the end of the film, thus making for an 'open door' ending (as in *Father* and *Underground*), or remains incomplete: the bride dies (Azra), the groom is killed (Ahmed), the bride commits suicide (Jelena), the groom drowns (Jovan), the bride runs away (Afrodita). If a married couple figure in the film, their wedding is not shown – we never see Meša and Sena's wedding (*Father*), nor Marko and Natalija's (*Underground*).

In *Underground* there are two weddings. From the onerous darkness of the first underground wedding Kusturica takes the viewers to the generous sunshine of the second one, on the Danube's shore. The first wedding, noisy and incongruous, ends up dispersed in a subterranean labyrinth. The other one, a happy and idealised replay, ends up floating away towards an unknown destination. Neither one of these weddings, however, comes to completion.

Underground's final wedding scene is a narrative device to gather everyone together for a culmination that cannot be compared with the standard intense eventfulness of an ordinary wedding. Rather, it is used to deliver a warning about an oblivious drifting away towards an uncertain future. This is the only wedding where undisturbed happiness reigns; but it also takes place on a utopian chunk of land floating away into the unknown. Even though the cellar wedding was tense and unsettling, it was the real one; its cheerful replay is only an elusive fairy-tale, a complex metaphor for the never-ending calamities of the Balkans.

Humour

Kusturica says that he has always been interested in making comedies, but that certain aspects of his personality make him end up with films that are closer to tragedy. He also likes the burlesque, by definition a genre that vulgarises the lofty and elevates the ordinary.

Kusturica knows a thing or two about the subtlety of Czech humour and puts this knowledge to use in his early films. In later ones he often makes the protagonists engage in self-irony and ridicule each other by playing with stereotypical images of themselves – his Romani protagonists call each other 'thieving Gypsy', and his Balkan protagonists mock themselves for being caught up in the grip of 'Balkan paranoia'.

But humour is culturally sensitive and does not always translate internationally. To compensate, there is quite a lot of universal slapstick-type *mise-en-scène* in Kusturica. In *Brides* there is a scene showing Martin standing on top of a ladder and repairing something on the front façade of the house. Two mischievous boys attack him. They shake him off the ladder and leave him hanging, holding on to the balcony banister. The same mischievous situation is re-staged in *Arizona*. Another favourite set-up, repeated in many films, is to show the protagonist skidding on a slippery surface and collapsing on his bum. In *Underground* it happens several times – Marko skids in front of a bathtub, Blacky skids while chasing Natalija, German soldiers slip up in front of Café Moscow. It is an important slapstick trope, a constant reminder of instability and the possible reversal of fortunes at every step.

Slapstick is subtly present from early on (the uncle in *Gypsies* is seen imitating Charlie Chaplin), but comes into prominence only in *Arizona* (the home movie of Uncle Leo). The longer version of *Underground* has a strong slapstick feel, with a whole subplot about Marko who abducts a train dressed as a bride. But slapstick-style scenes are also found in the shorter theatrical version: Blacky's farcical torture, for example, enhanced by Marko's break-in to the hospital and the ensuing vaudeville abduction. It is slapstick of the kind familiar from the early Mack Sennett comedies, but there are also elements reminiscent of Buster Keaton and Groucho Marx. Another aspect of the slapstick *mise-en-scène* is the French influence – of comedians like Fernandel, Bourvil, Michel Simon and Louis De Funès – which remains relatively little recognised and acknowledged but is stronger and more pervasive than the American one.

The slapstick effect is often endowed with a tragicomic dimension, best seen in the frequently used scene of the failed suicide. When committing suicide, Kusturica's protagonists prefer to do it by hanging, and as a rule they fail because they have selected an elastic bungee-type cord which makes them swinging up and down, looking silly and certainly not killing themselves (e.g. Grace in *Arizona*). Ankica, the distraught mistress in *Father*, tries to hang herself on the line in the bathroom, but all she accomplishes is the flushing of the toilet. After being refused Azra's hand in *Gypsies*, the heart-broken Perhan attempts to hang himself on a church bell, thus ringing the bell and failing to die. It is a trope seen earlier in Tati's classic *Jour de fête* (1949).

The failed suicide scene is an important means of stressing on the relativity of interpretation: what may seem a tragic move towards terminating one's own life can be turned upside down and have a joyful continuation. The burlesque subtext of the failed suicide scenes, however, also predetermines the impossibility of a tragic resolution or definitive narrative closure. In the first part of *Underground*, the suicidal Ivan hangs on an equally unreliable rope and is taken down by his brother Marko. Only towards the end of the film does Ivan manage to hang himself on a church bell, becoming probably the only one of Kusturica's protagonists who succeeds in committing suicide, thus signalling the gravity of the situation.

Creatures and gadgets

> I want to be surrounded in each movie with the elements that I like to work with.
>
> Kusturica, quoted in Kaufman, 1999

Similar to other auteurs, Kusturica uses a favourite set of objects that fill up the space with familiar signals. A chess set, a merry-go-round, a hammock, a well, a flat fish, a couple of mischievous kids, a sparkler and a threesome in a bed all have a prominent place in his image assortment. Truly self-referential, he lets the flat fish from *Arizona* be caught by Blacky and Jovan in *Underground* and hangs a portrait of Ahmed from *Gypsies* on Dadan's wall in *Black Cat*.

Little things – creatures and gadgets – combined with persistent narrative tropes (similar situations shot in identical ways), define Kusturica's narrative universe and ensure the stylistic unity of his films. The shoe, for example: removing or putting on a woman's shoe, more often by a man and occasionally by the woman herself, is an image found in every film. The high-heeled shoe, most often white (*Brides*, *Dolly Bell*, *Gypsies*) but also appearing in black (*Underground*) and pink (*Black Cat*), is an object of sexual signification, often treated as a fetish.

The intense cinematic interest in the human body, which often finds expression in close explorations of nudity, sex or violence, is not present in Kusturica. He rarely shows nudity and when he does, it is to create a memorable image (e.g. Azra tattooing herself in the water in *Gypsies*). Sex scenes do not involve naked bodies rubbing against one another and very little skin is seen altogether. Foreplay is often signified by visual tropes that involve feet – a man removing a woman's shoe, or the man's foot in socks stretched out and caressing the legs of the woman who is the object of his interest. When engaged in sexual intercourse, lovers are usually

The flat fish from *Arizona Dream* ends up caught by Blacky and Jovan in *Underground*

covered with something – a blanket in *Dolly Bell* and *Father* and a lace petti-
coat in *Arizona*.

Nothing like the aesthetic glorification of violence that is so popular with
other contemporary directors can be found in Kusturica. In the rare
instances when he shows bodily violence (e.g. the violent coercion of Perhan
into crime by Ahmed's people), he does not take advantage of its show value,
but rather depicts it as something ugly and wrong. Rape scenes (in *Dolly Bell*,
Gypsies and the long version of *Underground*) are usually set up with a frontal
take of the woman's torso and part of her face, half-standing and leaning
against something and being violated from behind. The rapist is barely seen,
the focus is on the woman who endures the violence. In the other prominent
scene involving violent sex, Meša's basement rape of Ankica, the woman is
also being violated while kept straight up against a wall.

The director is reputed to enjoy working with animals which appear in
almost all his pictures – pigeons and rabbits in *Dolly Bell*, turtles in *Arizona*.
They are omnipresent in the Gypsy films – geese, pigs, dogs, horses and
goats. The inhabitants of the underground also raise all sorts of animals
which share their confined space.

Perhan's closest friend in *Gypsies* is his turkey, which according to
Kusturica is a bird that enjoys special standing in Romani mythology. The
moment at which the uncle slaughters the turkey to make soup, Kusturica
indicated, was the turning point of the film, the end of Perhan's childhood
and the beginning of his maturity. The turkey, symbolising his soul, keeps
returning to Perhan's dreams and its white ghost appears to him at the
moment of his death. While tense when dealing with some of the actors, the
director appears happy and relaxed when working with the chimp Charlie
on *Underground* (as seen in the documentary *Shooting Days*, 1997).

An interest in animals combines notably with a love of technology and
gadgets. The father in *Dolly Bell* is fascinated by the achievements of technology, which confirm progress towards modernity and herald the imminent arrival of the perfect social order. Mirza, the older brother in *Father*,
creates animated sequences about parachutists and Ankica, the mistress, is
a pilot. The flying devices in *Arizona* suggest a fascination with person-
friendly technology, juxtaposed to the technology of the consumerist society

Kusturica appears happy and relaxed when working with the chimp Charlie on
Underground

symbolised by the Cadillac; there is a home movie suggesting the early use
of video. The Gypsies are shown to love gadgets, particularly Grga Pitić in
Black Cat, who is surrounded by complex machinery and uses all sorts of
smart contraptions and devices. But while clever mechanisms are in high
esteem, the surveillance technology that Marko deploys to enslave the cellar
population in *Underground* suggests its potential for oppression.

The extensive use of watch and clock imagery, appearing with ever-
increasing frequency in the later films, seems to be related to the director's
sense of the relativity of time. In *Underground* Marko is regularly seen
removing his watch in a symbolic gesture when he wants time 'halted',
whether for a philandering adventure or for a fight. As the issue is control
over time, the big clock in *Underground*'s cellar is continuously being
readjusted. The abundant watches and clocks in *Black Cat* seem to be there
to suggest the Romani's different attitude to time.

Another favourite object seen throughout these films is the mirror,
often set up so as to produce multiple reflections. In *Titanic*, Stjepan
is shown standing in front of a triple mirror, looking at his triplicate

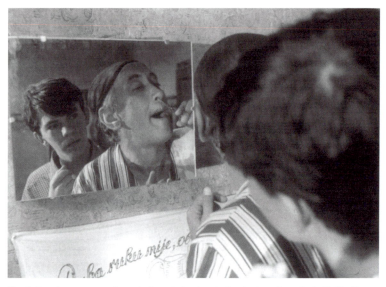

The father is seen wearing a hair net shaving in front of a mirror in both *Do You Remember Dolly Bell?* (above) and *When Father Was Away on Business*

reflection. Positioning a folding mirror for a rear view, in *Underground* Marko stares at the duplicate reflection of a prostitute's behind while she washes in the bathtub. A number of scenes in *Super 8 Stories* that take place in dressing rooms are shot at an angle that multiplies the mirror reflections of those present in the room. But the most memorable use of multiplied reflections remains the Russian roulette scene between Axel and Grace in *Arizona*.

Kusturica's use of mirrors is persistent and many more examples of scenes in front of mirrors can be quoted – the father wearing a hair net shaving in front of a mirror in *Dolly Bell* and *Father*, or scenes that take place in a room but are shot via their reflection in a mirror. Besides suggesting self-reflexivity, these images seem to strengthen other recurring motives in the director's work, particularly the double and multiple layers of occurrences.

The other arts

Westerners often tend to think of East Europeans as people who were raised on a diet of Soviet war movies. In fact, many East European intellectuals – and Kusturica is a typical case – enjoyed exposure to a wide range of works of art, sometimes even richer than that of the average Western intellectual. It included not only the best examples of the European tradition, but also of other cultures – from Russia to Latin America and Asia.

Literature appears to be of particular importance to Kusturica. His early films were adapted from literary sources and in later ones he used loose associations with literary works. Two of his unrealised projects were to be adaptations of classical literary prototypes: by Andrić and Dostoevsky.

The director's work is often classified as magical realist, but he does not seem to be interested in or influenced by Yugoslav magic realism, a well-developed branch of this literature (best-known for Milorad Pavić's 1988 *Hazarski Rečnik* [*Khazar Dictionary*]); only the influence of Latin American magical realism has been acknowledged. Kusturica has commented extensively on its affiliation with the Yugoslav mentality, of shared attitudes to rationality, morality and history. Gabriel García Márquez's novel *One Hundred Years of Solitude* was identified as a source of inspiration for *Gypsies*, even though no concrete elements of Márquez's work were brought into the film. Other authors Kusturica has mentioned include Carlos Fuentes, Jorge Luis Borges, Julio Cortázar and MarioVargas Llosa.

It is difficult to judge precisely to what extent Márquez defined Kusturica's magic realism. On the one hand, parallel with its success in the West, Latin American magic realist writing was extremely popular in the countries of the Balkans where it appeared in translation around the time of Márquez's Nobel Prize in 1982. On the other hand, magical elements are found throughout Balkan mythology and folklore and they have been extensively used within Yugoslav literature itself. It would be, therefore, misleading to describe the presence of fantasy quirks as a Latin American import, as these have been continuously present in the artistic output of the Balkans and no cross-cultural mediation was needed to discover and use them.

Why, then, has the director spoken more of Márquez's influence? Maybe because of his desire to communicate adequately with Western interviewers, who were more likely to know of this literary tradition than the Slavic one. Even though Márquez was neither the first nor only magical realist, it is his work that has come to be known worldwide as a synonym for magic realism and it is true that Latin American sensibilities have a lot in common with Balkan ones. The reference to Márquez is an appropriate one, even if it results in the neglect of some closer sources of inspiration.

Besides his favourite Andrić, Kusturica holds in high esteem Milos Crnjanski (1893–1977), particularly his 1921 novella *Dnevnik o Čarnojeviću/Diary about Carnojevic*, and the Sarajevan writer Meša Selimović (1910–1982). His preference for Russian literature is well documented. Besides his affection for Dostoevsky he has identified Chekhov and Gogol as his favourite authors. In early interviews Kusturica stressed that Czech literature influenced him more than Czech film, talking of his admiration for Bohumil Hrabal and Milan Kundera. From American literature he has mentioned the works of Charles Bukowski and Raymond Carver and from French, Marcel Proust and Albert Camus.

Unlike Fellini, Kusturica does not make sketches when planning his films. This is probably why he says he feels like a painter who paints with a camera. His imagery has been linked to that of Pieter Brueghel, Marc Chagall and occasionally Hieronymus Bosch. Brueghel's influence can be seen in his crowded compositions where many little events take place simultaneously, stories evolve in multiple layers and the actual central event may appear only as a fragment, as one among many in the semantic space of the painting (like in *Fall of Icarus* where the protagonist only appears in the corner of the frame). References to Chagall have been made mostly in relation to the levitation scenes. In either case – Brueghel or Chagall – the influence is not a direct one but is mediated through the films of Tarkovsky, whose imagery and aesthetics are much closer to the work of both painters.

It was a remark by Benjamin Halligan (2000) that first drew my attention to a more significant influence – that of Yugoslav naïvist painting. Giuseppe Ghigi (Boni, 1999, p. 38) also talks of a naïvist influence, revealed in Kusturica's interest in rituals, dreams and the uninterrupted circle of life and death.

And indeed, multiple layers of occurrences – flying figures, weddings and other gatherings, groups of people moving in all directions all the time – that seem chaotic and uncoordinated but supply unmatched dynamism often appear in the naïvists and Kusturica alike. The coexistence of people and animals is a key feature, and the same range of mostly domesticated (but sometimes wild) animals – turkeys, geese, deer and goats – is poeticised. The specific use of colour as spots, as first seen in the late impressionists, is also characteristic of the work of some Yugoslav naïvist painters, and similar colour combinations are found in the work of Petar Mandić and Vangel Naumovski, for example. It is possible that the naïvist effects in Kusturica come indirectly via his production designers, but there is no doubt that as far as painting is concerned the naïvist influence is a profound one.

Music is an integral part of Kusturica's films; since *Gypsies* the director has acknowledged the wealth of Balkan traditional music and has shown a persistent preference for folklore melodies arranged to contemporary rock rhythms. He has a taste for an eclectic fusion of adapted Gypsy tunes and rock and roll, of improvisation and careful orchestration. In his films he has used a combination of popular songs (often Italian or Spanish) and classical music (from composers such as Vivaldi and Dvořák). But his personal preferences are for rock music and performers like Sid Vicious and Lou Reed: 'Have you ever been to the concerts of *The Clash* or *The Sex Pistols*, whom I unfortunately never saw on stage?' Kusturica once asked. 'They never stop; it's a catharsis with no beginning and no end. You know, I play in a rock group and that gives me the best sensations in life' (Yarovskaya, 1997–8, p. 54).

Even though Kusturica is well-read and knowledgeable about a wide range of artistic works, there is a certain anti-intellectualism that characterises his *oeuvre*. It finds expression in his fascination with excess and kitsch and can be seen as an extension of his overall 'pagan' attitude and devotedness to the 'buddy' culture. No images of high art *à la* Tarkovsky or texts or scriptures *à la* Peter Greenaway figure in Kusturica's image inventory. Everything is more primitive, simple, more 'Balkan', endowed with a Fellinesque vitality that radically rejects cerebral and speculative rationality.

The protagonists in Kusturica's films rarely refer to literature and they are not normally seen reading books. If books appear, it is either as a frayed paperback on hypnosis (*Dolly Bell*) or an Italian Alan Ford comic (*Black Cat*). Unlike Tarkovsky, whose protagonists are regularly seen looking at paintings or prints reproduced in books, Kusturica's heroes rarely come in contact with fine art. Neither are they seen drawing or painting. But they make music all the time, involved with smaller or bigger bands – a rock group in *Dolly Bell*, a band of Mariachi in *Arizona Dream* and Gypsy brass bands in *Underground* and *Black Cat*. Kusturica likes to include interesting-looking instruments in the picture, and besides the accordion (played by Mirza in *Father*, Perhan in *Gypsies* and Grace in *Arizona*), his preferences seem to be the tuba, the trumpet and the harmonica.

As far as theatre is concerned, Kusturica is more interested in theatrical elements in real life – rehearsing and putting on a show, most often to manipulate and deceive – than in formal stage performances. His focus is on popular spectacles, traditional ceremonies, rituals and festivities, and rarely on theatrical art as such.

Most of all, however, Kusturica's protagonists like going to the movies. They like acting out scenes from movies and they are occasionally involved in making movies, because this is a way to 're-double the sense of reality', as the director says in the press kit for *Underground*.

Influences and intertextuality

In his autobiography, Fellini said that he rarely went to the movies; he did not really know the cinema classics and never paid much attention to camera movements or the set-up of a scene. In this respect, Kusturica is very different. Not only has he seen a substantial number of film classics; he has also paid close attention to their mastery, to the camera movements and to the scenes' structure.

Kusturica has repeatedly stressed his preference for classical cinema; to him everything in contemporary film is derived from the classics. In interviews he has named Fellini, Tarkovsky, Capra, Buñuel, Ford and Renoir as his major cinematic mentors, and has identified Italian neo-realism, French poetic realism and Russian cinema as key influences. 'I feel closer to Fellini, to Renoir or to Buñuel than to the majority of films that I see nowadays,' he said (Ciment, 1993, p. 24).

Besides identifying general influences on Kusturica, here I have to undertake a slightly different exploration, a fuller analysis of what have come to be known as Kusturica's 'make-overs'. It concerns the frequent instances where the director uses images and scenes from other films which he replicates on the canvas of his own.

It was the film scholar Andrew Horton who first remarked on these 'make-overs'. As early as 1988, when discussing *Father*, Horton talked about Kusturica's familiarity with classical Hollywood cinema and said that he 'could document a tiresome list of stylistic elements that suggests Kusturica's debt to such a cinema' (1988, p. 71). He did not do it in that instance, but such a list nonetheless materialised at a later point, in a text published in 1998. Here Horton spoke of direct and indirect references to over forty directors, 'ranging from the surrealism of Luis Buñuel to the straightforward, clean, narrative visual style of John Ford'. He took time to identify some of the 'make-overs' in *Gypsies*, mostly those coming from American and Yugoslav cinema. He must also have noticed other 'make-overs' – from Italian, French and Russian films – but he did not discuss them, probably in order to avoid overwhelming the reader. He wrote:

> Kusturica, like a gypsy, has stolen from everyone, including from his native
> Bosnian and Yugoslav tradition for folk surrealism and magic realism. [...]
> Taken together, all of these intertextual, Hollywood, European and other
> national cinematic 'quotes' strongly suggest that Kusturica wishes his film to
> be taken as a member of a club that includes not only Hollywood but world
> cinema itself.
>
> 1998, p. 181

There are instances of 'make-overs' in earlier films, but by the time of *Gypsies* they become a permanent element of Kusturica's work and have persisted ever since.

In this context, we need to distinguish three aspects of influence and intertexuality. First, there are the overall aesthetic influences, most of which have been widely acknowledged. Second, there are the 'nods' or 'homages', those easily recognisable intertextual references to elements of other films that the director has inserted in his own. And third, there are the 'make-overs', nearly literal re-stagings of scenes from other films. I will trace these three levels of influences and intertextuality by organising the material around national cinemas.

From Yugoslav cinema

All Kusturica films contain direct 'nods' to a range of popular Yugoslav cinematic works, all easily recognised by domestic audiences. The 'nods' range from Aleksandar Petrović's *I Even Met Happy Gypsies* to Šijan's *Who is Singing*

Flock of geese in Aleksandar Petrović's *I Even Met Happy Gypsies* (1967)

Out There for the Gypsy-themed films, or from Hajrudin Krvavac's *Valter brani Sarajevo* (*Walter Defends Sarajevo*, 1972) to popular TV series like *Written Off* (1974) for *Underground*.

Živojin Pavlović, a leading figure of the Yugoslav 'black wave', is often identified by Kusturica as one of his favourite directors. Like Pavlović's, Kusturica's films also evolve in the periphery, in areas with no authentic urban population, and they are preoccupied with the migration to the city and the ambitions and moral codes of the people of the margins (Bertellini, 1996, p. 14). Pavlović's *oeuvre* is cross-referenced in a scene of *Gypsies*, when one of Ahmed's brothers is killed in an outhouse (a quote from Pavlović's 1967 *Kad budem mrtav i beo* [*When I am Pale and Dead*]).

The references to Dušan Makavejev are even more numerous. Examples include the neighbour in *Father*, who is played by the actress Eva Ras and is called Ilonka. (Ilonka was the protagonist of Makavejev's 1967 *Ljubavni slu-čaj ili tragedija službenice P.T.T.* [*Love Affair of the Case of the Missing Switchboard Operator*], played by Ras). The orgon camera of Makavejev's 1971 *WR: Misterije organisma* (*WR: Mysteries of Organism*) is seen in the cellar in the long version of *Underground*. There are also numerous references and quotes from the work of members of the Yugoslav Prague group (mostly Grlić and Paskaljević), to which Kusturica believed himself to belong during the early stages of his career. In *Gypsies*, for example, Perhan and Azra go to a makeshift open-air cinema and watch a film featuring actor Miki Manojlović in a sexually charged scene from Rajko Grlić's *Samo jednom se ljubi* (*You Only Love Once*, 1981).

Weddings and animals were central images for the late Ivica Matić, whose only film, the lyrical *Žena s krajolikom* (*Woman with a Landscape*, 1975), was a strong influence and from whose script Kusturica filmed *Brides* in 1978. The flying bride was first seen in Ante Babaja's *Breza* (*Birch Tree*, 1967), a film that supplied one of Kusturica's poetic tropes.

From Czech cinema

The influence of leading film-makers of the Czech new wave – Jiří Menzel, Miloš Forman, Vojtěch Jasný, Jaromil Jireš, Ján Němec – is strongly felt in Kusturica's earlier work but has been little acknowledged, and these names are almost never mentioned in Western interviews alongside the officially identified influences.

The Czecho-Slovak lineage is clearly felt in the subtle humour of the early films, as well as in the way their narrative is structured. Kusturica's use of multiple layers of occurrences within the same frame is similar to Juraj Jakubisko's, a director often described as the Slovak Fellini. Both share an interest in surreal elements, also characteristic of the work of Ján Němec. Vojtěch Jasný's 1968 *Všichni dobří rodáci* (*All My Good Countrymen*), set at the same period as *Father*, also tells how the private lives of his protagonists were affected by the highly politicised times. Like *Father*, Jaromil Jireš' 1968 *Žert* (*The Joke*), based on Kundera's novel, also revolves around an innocent joke that has grave repercussions for the protagonist. Besides the similarity of the plot, *Father* and *The Joke* have a lot in common in the

Miloš Forman's *Loves of a Blonde* (1965)

way they reach their resolution. In both films, the protagonists have to settle private accounts in a public place: in *The Joke* the setting is a street celebration in a provincial town, in *Father* it is a wedding. In both films, viewers are aware of the complex background and suppressed tensions, an awareness that makes these seemingly ordinary scenes emotionally saturated and explosive.

The restaurant scene in *Father*, where women in white blouses sit on tables waiting for the men to initiate contact, is directly out of Miloš Forman's *Loves of a Blonde*. The way people make music in *Dolly Bell* is reminiscent of Forman's early music documentary *The Competition* (1963), and the officials planning activities for the young people and the scenes of dancing at the youth club recall Forman's *Firemen's Ball*. The empty streets and the women looking out of windows in *Bar Titanic* replicate the flashbacks of Ján Němec's *Démanty Noci* (*Diamonds of the Night*, 1963). Elements of Mento Papo's behaviour in the same film parallel those of Josef Kroner's character, Tono, from *The Shop on Main Street* (Ján Kádár/Elmar Klos, 1965). The ending to Jiří Menzel's *Closely Watched Trains* where the protagonist falls dead on top of a moving train is directly replicated by Perhan's death in *Time of the Gypsies*. *Gypsies* also contains a make-over of an episode from the Slovak Roma film *Ruzové sny* (*Rose-Tinted Dreams*, 1976) by Dusan Hanak.

From Russian cinema

At FAMU Kusturica was extensively exposed to many Soviet classics. He has readily spoken of the influence of the 'Russians', mentioning Tarkovsky and Vsevolod Pudovkin. Asked about Dovzhenko, whose influence is sensed in the scene of the sunflower field in *Black Cat*, he said that it was *Zemlja* (*Earth*, 1930) that taught him how to treat nature and the place of the human being within landscape (Ciment, 1998, p. 21).

The profound influence of Tarkovsky is evident in virtually every film of Kusturica. It is not an ideological one as the metaphysical quests of Tarkovsky's protagonists are far removed from the mundane ones of Kusturica's characters. Neither is it shown in respect of narrative, as Kusturica's dynamic eventfulness is quite unlike Tarkovsky's minimalist

Tarkovsky is paid a 'homage' every time a white horse crosses the frame in *Underground*

My Name is Ivan (1962) is referenced at various places in *Underground*, most notably in the nearly literal reconstruction of Ivan's dream of his mother's death

contemplation. The influence is a purely formal one, discovered in the transplantation of Tarkovskean imagery and in the camera work. As far as imagery is concerned, Tarkovsky is paid a 'homage' every time a white horse or a stray dog crosses the frame in Kusturica, as well as in most scenes involving water, rain and windows. Scenes from almost all Tarkovsky's films have been replicated in Kusturica's. A listing of all examples would take more space than I can afford here, so I will identify only some of the concrete 'make-overs'.

According to Vecchi, Tarkovsky's first feature-length film *My Name is Ivan* is explicitly used in *Father*'s ending, but also in *Arizona Dream*'s oneiric opening (1999, pp. 44, 17). *My Name is Ivan* is replicated in all the scenes that represent someone running and splashing through water. There are extensive references throughout *Underground*, most notably in the nearly literal reconstruction of Ivan's dream of his mother's

Running and splashing through water as seen in *Andrei Rublev* (1965)

Tarkovsky's *The Mirror* (1974)

Kusturica's *Arizona Dream* (1993)

A scene from *Black Cat, White Cat:* 'Zéro de conduite'?

death next to a well, here re-made in the episode where Natalija descends to the cellar.

The classic camera work of Vadim Yusov in *Andrei Rublev* (1965) has been strictly replicated in the many elaborately staged scenes relying on complex vertical and horizontal camera movements in *Gypsies*. The best example is the river scene of the St George's Day celebration, directly reminiscent of the pagan river celebration in Tarkovsky. Another one is the 'magic realist' scene where within the same take Azra and Perhan are first seen in front of a limestone oven, then on its top and then back down – a take constructed in a way very similar to the camera work of the famous bell sequence in *Rublev*.

Elements from *The Mirror* are repeatedly replicated in Kusturica's films, from *Dolly Bell* to *Underground*. Not only in the instances of levitation and telekinesis, but also in all those situations where water is poured over one's head (Dolly Bell's, Muzafer's in *Father*) or where the protagonists (Dino, Axel, Natalja) look out of a window into the rain outside. *The Mirror*'s and

Sacrifice's influence is also seen in the combination of rain and fire: in *Gypsies*, Perhan's home is set on fire in pouring rain; in *Arizona*, lightning sets the nearby tree on fire amidst a downpour at the film's climax.

Perhan's telekinetic abilities are like those of the girl from *Stalker* and some of the shots of his sister Danira in a scarf replicate the same girl's profiles in Tarkovsky. *Nostalghia* (1983) contains a scene of a levitating pregnant woman, like Azra.

Paolo Vecchi (1999, p. 45) and John Orr (2000, pp. 59–60) talk of a Paradzhanov influence, but I believe it is more the result of a similarity of sensibility between the cinemas of the Balkans and the Caucasus. Other, more remote, Russian influences are the epics of Andrei Mikhalkov-Konchalovsky (*Sibiriada* [*Siberiade*,1979]) and Elem Klimov (*Idi i smotri* [*Come and See*,1985]).

From French cinema

Kusturica has repeatedly stressed the strong influence of French poetic realism, and the directors he names most often are Jean Vigo and Jean Renoir. *L'Atalante*, in particular, has been identified as an endless source of inspiration. Jean Renoir's influence can mostly be found in the staging of multi-layered scenes, as seen in *La Règle du jeu* (*The Rules of the Game*, 1939), but also in a certain kind of humour, *à la* Boudu.

Another French influence is early Jacques Tati, elements of whose *Jour de fête* have been made over in *Gypsies* and *Black Cat*. When discussing Kusturica, critics have also made references to the work of Cocteau, René Clair and Godard (whose 1959 *À bout de souffle* [*Breathless*] Kusturica has also quoted as a key influence), as well as Truffaut.

Kusturica has also expressed his high respect for the celebrated Yugoslav-born French artist Enki Bilal, a cult figure in the world of comic strips, who ventured briefly into directing (Ostria, 1994 p. 81). Bilal's *Bunker Palace Hotel* (1989) is characterised by the same grim visual style as *Underground* and also revolves around keeping refugees in a cellar. Featuring a cast of renowned French and Yugoslav actors and shot in Belgrade, the film is an anti-utopian vision set in an imaginary dictatorship where a group of people hide in a bunker from a rebellion raging outside.

From Italian cinema

First of all, there is Fellini, whose influence expands far beyond the atmospheric light, the scaffolds, the puffballs, the wind and dust. In 1999 Kusturica said that he is proud of having discovered how Fellini made films and that he is using the same 'little tricks, like a magician who sees one circus and goes into another to work'. He identifies three of these specific features: First, the excitement that comes from every character one encounters; second, the incredible architecture of the scenes; third, the dominant 'Mediterranean, paganistic vision of life' (Fuller, 1999, p. 69).

Quotes from many Fellini films are scattered throughout Kusturica's work. Having quoted *La Strada* (1954) as one of his favourite films, for example, Kusturica makes Joža, the neighbour's boy in *Father*, practice tearing a chain with his chest, like Zampanò. In *Gypsies*, Romani children run after the car that takes Perhan and Danira away in a scene replicating the Gelsomina's sisters running after the departing vehicle in *La Strada*.

But it is probably the colours and atmosphere of *Amarcord* that have had the most persistent presence in Kusturica's work. It is noticeable in a range of techniques and images – the way dark scenes are lit, the extended use of a whirlwind blowing little white feathers around against the background of an unsettling soundtrack, the accordion player, the on-screen musicians – all features found in most of Kusturica's films. Then, there is the man who addresses the audience at the opening (as in *Gypsies*) and at the close (as in *Underground*), the boy who hypnotises a big bird (like Perhan in *Gypsies*), the mother epitomising domesticity (like the wives played by Mirjana Karanović in *Father* and *Underground*), Gradisca, the local beauty, her numerous affairs and red dress (like Natalija in *Underground*), the wedding set in open air (like the one in *Father*) and more.

Italian neo-realism also has left an imprint on Kusturica; he often speaks of Luchino Visconti's *Senso* (1955) as a film of crucial importance for the development of his artistic views. Vittorio de Sica's *Ladri di bicilette* (*Bicycle Thieves*, 1948) and *Miracle in Milan* are not only recognised influences, but have also been cross-referenced. Several elements of *Milan* are made-over in *Gypsies*, while *Bicycle Thieves* strongly influences the child's point of view narrative of *Father*, as well as the image inventory of the film.

Azra in *Gypsies*?;
Edvige in *Miracle in
Milan* (1951)

De Sica's work, however, has a strong proletarian commitment and its political overtones are very different from the politics of Kusturica, whose concerns have little in common with de Sica's overt Marxism.

The spaghetti Westerns of Sergio Leone have been a great influence. The
expressive faces and close-ups in Kusturica are much more like those of
Leone than those of Fellini. The way some Gypsies look in *Black Cat* is reminiscent of Leone's bandits: Grga Pitić looks like Lee Van Cleef, Blacky in
Underground is a cross-breed between Eli Wallach and Gian Maria Volontè.
A famous train scene from *Once Upon a Time in the West* (1968), showing a
man on top of a moving train leaning over to look through the window into
a compartment, is re-made by Kusturica at least twice, in *Gypsies* and in
Underground. Leone's *A Fistful of Dynamite* (1972) explores the union
between politics and crime disguised by revolutionary rhetoric. Here, a pair

of buddies (a robber and an idealistic politician) get involved in a series of adventures and engage in many situations of which the actions of Blacky and Marko in *Underground* are directly reminiscent.

From German cinema

Volker Schlöndorff's *The Tin Drum*, based on the novel by Günther Grass, seems to have been a direct influence on *Father*. The films share a similar view on history's impact on the individual and they both use a child's point of view as a narrative strategy. *The Tin Drum* is set among Kashubians in the peripheral city of Danzig (Gdansk), *Father*, among Muslims in the peripheral city of Sarajevo. Further common features are the numerous vertical entrances and actions structured around the divide of below and above. In both films, for example, we have a scene in which a child under the table (Oskar Mazerath and Malik respectively) observes a man's foot in a sock caressing a woman's leg.

Igor Krstic (1999) discovered numerous textual parallels between *Underground* and Fassbinder's *Lili Marleen* (1981) and *Die Ehe der Maria Braun*

The Tin Drum (1979) and *Arizona Dream*: sheltered under skirts

(*The Marriage of Maria Braun*, 1979). According to him, *Maria Braun* is also referenced in the radio broadcast accompaniment to the last ten minutes of *Father*. Kusturica appeared as a man dealing in arms in *Underground* and Fassbinder as a black marketeer in *Maria Braun*. Vecchi spoke of influences from Joseph von Sternberg's *Der Blaue Engel* (*Blue Angel*, 1930). Other critics have made references to the hands of the clock from Fritz Lang's *Metropolis* (1926), to Wenders' *Paris, Texas*, as well as to Herzog and Syberberg. Kusturica explicitly underlined how he loved Wenders' work (1993, p. 35). The leading narrative premise of DEFA's classic *Jakob der Lügner* (*Jakob the Liar*, 1974, dir. Frank Beyer) is used in *Underground*.

From British cinema

Compared to the other European countries, Kusturica's work is probably least known in the UK. Correspondingly, Kusturica has only occasionally been influenced by British cinema. Notable examples include Terry Gilliam (*Time Bandits*, 1981) and Carol Reed (*The Third Man*).

From American cinema

It is probably because critics are most familiar with American cinema that so many American parallels in Kusturica's films have been noticed so widely. There have been references to the work of Buster Keaton, Leo McCarey, Charlie Chaplin, Frank Capra, Ernst Lubitsch, Michael Curtiz, Tod Browning, Howard Hawks, Busby Berkeley, Alfred Hitchcock, the Marx brothers, Charles Laughton, Elia Kazan, Sam Pekinpah, Robert Altman, Arthur Penn, Peter Bogdanovich, Roman Polanski, Miloš Forman, Michael Cimino, Woody Allen, David Lynch, Tim Burton, Alex Cox, Quentin Tarantino and Jim Jarmush. The work of all these men has been alluded to in one way or another, be it with a 'hommage' like the one to Robert Flaherty's *Nanook of the North* (1922) in *Arizona*, or with an indirect 'nod' like the title of Billy Wilder's *Kiss Me, Stupid* (1964), a line thrown into a casual conversation in *Black Cat*. *Underground*'s main plotline is reminiscent of Gottfried Reinhardt's *Situation Hopeless... But Not Serious* (1965), where a German (Alec Guinness) keeps captive American soldiers (Mike Connors, Robert Redford) in his cellar after the war is over by making up news reports.

Kusturica has identified John Ford as a major American influence. According to Horton 'there is more of John Ford's style in Kusturica's work than there is of even Coppola, Buñuel, or any other cinematic father figure' (1998, pp. 180–81). He sees the ending of *Dolly Bell*, where the family is seen loading belongings onto the truck and preparing to drive away, as a direct make-over of the ending of *Grapes of Wrath* (1940) and identifies many other instances where one can clearly feel the influence of *Stagecoach* (1939) or other Ford films. Michel Ciment (1998, p. 19) has also remarked on the influence of Ford, referring to lesser-known early films such as *Judge Priest* (1934) and *Steamboat Round the Bend* (1935).

In *Gypsies*, Perhan is seen standing in front of a poster featuring Orson Welles. This is yet another 'hommage' to a director who is a key influence, particularly with films like *Citizen Kane* (1941), *The Magnificent Ambersons* (1942), *The Stranger*, *The Lady from Shanghai* and *Othello* (1952), an influence which translates in Kusturica's use of dramatic shadows, clocks, mirror images, watches and ornate interiors, as well as his multi-layered *mise-en-scène*.

Apocalypse Now (1979) referenced in *Underground*

Martin Scorsese and Francis Ford Coppola rank among Kusturica's favourite American directors, and their cinematic vision has had an overall impact on his style. Kusturica has paid homage to Scorsese's *Raging Bull* in *Arizona Dream* and to *Taxi Driver* in *Black Cat*. References to Coppola's *Apocalypse Now* are found in *Underground*, and according to Andrew Horton (1998) *Gypsies* can be considered to be a remake of Coppola's *Godfather* (1971) and *Godfather II* in that it replicates the story of the making of a reluctant crime lord.

The aesthetic of the early films of the Coen brothers (*Blood Simple*, 1983; *Raising Arizona*, 1987) and Gus van Sant (*Drugstore Cowboy*, 1989; *My Own Private Idaho*) is closer to Kusturica than that of the films of other American directors of his generation.

From international cinema

Kusturica has readily listed the Spaniard Buñuel among the leading influences on his work. The dream sequences in *Gypsies*, for example, seem to be directly inspired by oneiric material in *Los Olvidados* (1950).

Even though Kusturica is said not to like *Czlowiek z marmuru* (*Man of Marble*, 1977), he identified Andrzej Wajda as one of his favourite directors (Bouineau, 1993, p. 77). Inspiration for *Underground* comes from *Kanal*; the inverted crucifix in the third part of *Underground* replicates the inverted Christ of Wajda's *Ashes and Diamonds*. Ahmed's wedding in *Gypsies* is shot in a way reminiscent of Wajda's *Wesele* (*Wedding*, 1973).

A range of other international directors are also alluded to. The hairdo and the dress of the big singer from *Black Cat* replicate the outfit of Aki Kaurismaki's *Leningrad Cowboys Go America* (1989). A lovemaking scene involving Gypsies, water and a river shore from Moldovan Emil Loteanu's *Tabor ukhodit v nebo* (*Gypsies Are Found Near Heaven*), a favourite at the 1977 Belgrade Film Festival, may be the source of inspiration for the river lovemaking scene in *Gypsies*. Some general stylistic influences come from directors Pedro Almodovar and Jane Campion.

*   *   *

The list can be extended, but this is not the place for a complete catalogue of all the 'nods' and 'make-overs' in Kusturica's films. It is such a key device in his work, however, that it merits some more discussion. It is possible to tell, when watching his films, that some moment represents yet another 'make-over', only sometimes it is difficult to identify where it comes from.

The difficulty in identifying the full extent of 'make-overs' is due to the specialist segmentation of film scholarship. While one observer may know most of the East European sources, others may detect more references to Italian or to American cinema that they know better. One thing is certain – Kusturica only makes-over the work of recognised cinematic masters. Thus, he demonstrates an excellent background in cinema, in fact better than that of many film scholars who remain compartmentalised and rarely look beyond their narrow research field.

Like his *Arizona* character Paul Leger, Kusturica enjoys re-enacting scenes from a range of films that he has seen and liked. The resulting eclecticism has 'become a specific element of Kusturica's idiosyncratic style' (Horton, 1998, p. 178). Bringing together so many diverse elements from various films also accounts for the absence of a clearly articulated stylisation and for the post-modern feel of his films. Rather than building up one stylistic line, Kusturica replicates many different ones.

The way the 'make-overs' appear is another issue. In some cases they strictly follow the prototype, in others it is just a rough reconstruction by memory. In some cases the 'make-overs' rely on elements of the *mise-en-scène*. In others, they extend to the props, the camera work and even to the montage, thus involving the set designer, the cameraman and the editor.

There are two possible interpretative frameworks for this somewhat overwhelming abundance of 'homages', 'nods' and 'make-overs'. First, the one that seeks to reveal the Bakhtinian and even Nietzschean dimension of his poetics, favoured by Bertellini (1996, p. 98). Indeed, the categories of intertextuality, pastiche, collage and bricolage all work nicely in this case. Bertellini talks of Kusturica's work as an attempt to create and capitalise on a Balkan ethnography, whose vernacular language is microhistorical, regional and corporeal and which through his continuous multi-referencing takes on a sort of Vichian perspective on life and death and on the topos of *Bildungsroman* (1996, pp. 98–102).

The second interpretative line has been offered by Horton who speaks of 'cinematic border-crossings' and 'cross-cultural makeovers' that allow the director to address an international range of viewers who operate within a system of different cultural connotations. By making over elements from international films, Horton believes, Kusturica is able to strengthen his communicative power and provide a wider access to his idiosyncratic Yugoslav stories. He purposefully uses elements that are familiar to domestic viewers, but also elements that are familiar to international ones, thus speaking simultaneously to multiple international audiences. Kusturica's versatile background plays an important role here, as he can address concrete issues that concern him and at the same time communicate with a diverse international audience by sending out these little signals in the forms of 'nods' and 'make-overs'. Horton compares the strategy of 'makeovers' to Groucho Marx's 'asides', jokes that are missed by many but are a sheer pleasure for those who 'get' them.

While I believe that either one of these interpretations is good enough in itself, I think it is also important to keep in mind Kusturica's specific stance on the issue of influences and intertextuality. In a range of interviews (particularly earlier ones) he took care to tell the interviewer that a certain film or a director had 'unconsciously' or 'coincidentally' influenced him. Later on, he repeatedly talked of general influences and has acknowledged the 'nods', but has spoken of the 'make-overs' only if asked. 'Your mentioning of Dovzhenko's name in regard to this scene,' he tells Ciment who asks him about a concrete example from *Black Cat*, 'makes me realise a relationship of which I never thought up until today' (1998, p. 21). When Ciment asks him if certain early John Ford films influenced him, Kusturica replies that, when preparing to shoot *Black Cat*, he indeed ordered and watched a number of lesser-seen John Ford movies (p. 19). Then he comes up with a general explanation, tracing all these instances back to film school, which 'allows you to see films without knowing what effects, unconsciously, they will have on you a quarter of a century later' (p. 21).

Four
The Ideology

Kusturica's style has grown more lavish and intense with each film, but his understanding of categories like the family, the community and the historical process has remained largely the same. His main interest is in the life cycle of a male protagonist and in particular in the tribulations of growing up. When moral and social concerns cross paths with the main line of investigation in his narratives, they nonetheless remain secondary to the prevailing coming-of-age angle, one that seems to be informed by the director's overpowering egocentrism. His plots unravel as face-to-face confrontations within extended families; his interest is focused mostly on the neighbourhood power mechanics, resulting in an idiosyncratic understanding of social processes and, ultimately, history.

Back in 1976, talking of *The Third Man*, Marc Ferro undertook to show how a film's political meaning could be hidden behind mythic references and style and insisted that a distinction be made between narrative technique and style and a director's ideology.

In Kusturica's case, similarly, admiration for his abundant and exuberant artistry and esteem for the overwhelming richness of his visual style have somewhat obscured the understanding of his ideology. This is why it is of particular importance for this investigation that artistry and ideology be considered separately. Only such an approach allows us to adequately discuss Kusturica's films in relation to larger social categories like religion, history and communism, and to consider the social significance of Kusturica's takes on patriarchy, nationalism and populism.

In this chapter I will discuss the most important elements of Kusturica's way of looking at things – his views on religion and morality, on history and communism, on Yugoslavia and the Big Powers, on the community and extended family and on an individual's life cycle – as it has found expression in his films and his public statements.

One of the issues that, due to space limitations, I will not be considering here is Kusturica's view of the Gypsies. A serious exploration of this topic would need to look into why, given that Kusturica is the author of two of the best-known films about Gypsies and adored by many Yugoslav Romanies, he is not involved with public advocacy on Romani social causes. The answer, I believe, can be found in the general treatment of Romanies in Balkan cinema, where Gypsy plots have regularly been embraced as a winning recipe for the self-exoticisation willingly sought by many Balkan filmmakers. [*]

The second area that I will leave out is a discussion of the director's alleged 'misogyny' (Rayns, 1996, p. 53) and of his one-dimensional portrayal of women. With the exception of the nurturing and buoyant Hatidža, the Gypsy matriarch, Kusturica's women can be divided into several categories, ranging from the mainstay of domesticity (a housewife who grumbles over her husband's philandering but nonetheless shines his shoes and cooks large breakfasts to cure his hangover), the opportunistic beauty, the blonde object of desire (whose top priority is nonetheless to marry a well-positioned man) and the virginal bride (a static icon with primarily visual functions). To the majority of critics (coincidentally male), the most memorable images of women in Kusturica are those of brides floating and fluttering. As a female critic, I am more inclined to remember Marko planting a carnation in the prostitute's arse in *Underground*, the enormous singer whose act is to extract nails with her bottom, or the mawkish girls in Dadan's entourage in *Black Cat*. Where he comes from, Kusturica says, people are not bothered to look so much into the distinction between the sexes and 'things are as they are' (Bouineau, 1993, pp. 46 and 48) thus reinforcing a disturbing status quo in gender relations that requires critical examination.

Kusturica's work is rich in symbolic imagery begging for a psychoanalytical interpretation. Writers such as Horton (1988, 1998), Grünberg (1996), Žižek (1997), Yarovskaya (1997–8), Krstic (1999), Levi (2001) and others

---

[*] See my *Cinema of Flames*, 2001, chs 2 and 11.

Marko, carnation and a prostitute in *Underground*

have treated selected aspects of it from the point of view of psychoanalysis. A systematic psychoanalytical study of his entire *oeuvre*, besides looking into biographical material, would need to investigate the range of unrealised Oedipal confrontations that are present throughout the earlier work of the director, the rich symbolic texture of the dream sequences, as well as the scenes structured around the opposition of above and below.

All these areas of investigation are beyond the scope of the current work. Kusturica's views on other important topics will be discussed here in a structure reminiscent of concentric circles – from the general issues of transcendence and history down to the intimate spheres of family and the individual.

Transcendence

Kusturica's treatment of religion is not marked by an intellectually and emotionally exhausting spiritual quest for higher meaning, as we know it from the work of other directors. Even though formally influenced by Tarkovsky, Kusturica has no interest in the transcendental examinations of things like the nature of the Orthodox Holy Trinity, as seen in *Andrei Rublev*. He is not particularly disturbed by religious hypocrisy, so the mockery of the Church that is so typical of Fellini is not present in his films either. Even the instances of blasphemy in Kusturica do not come across as particularly out-rageous, maybe because his protagonists are not much preoccupied with issues of faith and transcendence. Ivan's blasphemous act of hanging him-self on a church bell in *Underground* is meant to suggest that he has given up on God. The same level of despair is encoded by the inverted figure of Christ, hanging upside down on a crucifix in the last part of *Underground*.

The director is interested in religion as a human practice, not as meta-physics. The range of religious practices shown in his films comes across more as the ethnography of everyday existence rather than as an exploration of faith and transcendence. Contrary to the view of the Balkans as a region marked by religious intolerance, here religions coexisted in happy syn-cretism marked by an overall pagan attitude. Kusturica has done a lot to rep-resent this syncretism: Mento Papo's Sarajevo pub in *Bar Titanic* is frequented by men of all local denominations, and his Croat Catholic lover Agata does not seem to have any problem with Mento's Jewishness. All faiths coexist in *Underground*'s cellar where the inhabitants are shown prac-tising a range of religious rituals. Grga Pitić in *Black Cat* wears a medallion that combines a Star of David, a Cross and a Crescent all in one.

A religious syncretism, however, is best shown in *Gypsies*. Perhan's fam-ily is formally Christian: his first dream takes place on the celebration of St George's Day in May, an important holiday within the Orthodox tradition; the central image of his second dream is the Catholic cathedral in Milan. But the grandmother also talks of going to a mosque in her attempt to save his ailing mother, and Ahmed's family is Muslim. At the opening of the film a man tells a folk tale about Gypsy dealings with God, and the Romani cos-mology involving a gallery of deities such as Sun and Moon, Earth and Ocean features prominently in other stories told in the film. It gives it all a syn-cretic flair, a breath of paganism that reigns over Gypsy religiosity.

The other side of Kusturica's celebratory 'paganism' is the absence of religious discourse, an absence that effectively removes any concern with radical issues of morality from his ideological universe. Dostoevsky has

Underground (left) and *Ashes and Diamonds* (Andrzej Wajda, 1958) (below): inverted crucifix

often been named among Kusturica's most important influences. When it comes to issues of religion and morality, however, one wonders precisely where the Dostoevsky lineage is in Kusturica's ideology. For the Russian writer, the crisis of faith and morality was a leading concern. Dostoevsky's disoriented and suffering protagonists are bound to the eternal search for superior will and meaning, they are engaged in an infinite and tragic questioning of the boundaries of moral order. They desperately need God, because they know that without God everything would be permissible, and because the very idea of a Universe without an organising principle leads to anxiety and disorientation.

The absence of God as an ultimate moral regulator does not create an intense feeling of moral emptiness for Kusturica's protagonists, who do not seem to experience the need of transcendentally positioned ethical norms (a need that informs Dostoevsky's *oeuvre*). Kusturica's treatment of moral issues is much closer to straightforward pragmatism, according to which the defining principle of morality is to act in a way that would mitigate adverse circumstances while minimising the damage caused to others.

Kusturica's protagonists are effectively spared the burden of soul-searching quests and revelations. In the few instances where they are preoccupied with higher truths they are exposed as simpletons operating with profane versions of sophisticated ideologies (e.g. the extended mockery of simplified Marxism in *Dolly Bell*). They suffer from political oppression but they do not martyr themselves over high ethical principles.

Thus, classic moral dilemmas are not at the centre of Kusturica's attention and the distinction between good and evil is never clear-cut. His characters do not suffer the agony of eternal moral doubt and self-flagellation, as do the protagonists of Tarkovsky or Bergman. To some extent, this is because Kusturica's views of agency are different. As his protagonists so often have to adjust to circumstances, their morality is reactive and opportunistic. They are not at liberty to reflect on moral decisions: they have to adjust urgently, their choices imposed by the flow of events where the will of the stronger prevails. The moral defences of the individual are being mobilised to rebuff concrete assaults of fate, building around categories of betrayal and revenge in an eventful narrative space where not much time is left for reflection on ethics in principle. Take Meša in *Father*: in his subordinate situation he is deprived of agency, and the most he can do is react to what he is confronted with. He could try resisting (and perish) but he makes the more realistic choice of adjusting. In such a social climate, even children are crystal clear about the power of pretence and the need to tell lies: Malik knows that the family friend sings Mexican songs because, unlike Russian or German ones, these are perceived as apolitical and 'safe'.

This relativism of ethical standards is taken to a logical extreme in *Underground*. Here, a Byzantine mentality and extreme opportunism blur all clear-cut moral considerations. In the context of economic and political instability and insecurity in the Balkans, the politics of petty survivalism and parasitism is seen as not only justifiable, but logical. There are no clear boundaries between swindling and trading, between victimisers and victims and no moral limits for those who have decided to survive, even at the cost of appropriating the freedom of others.

Excruciating questions about what is morally right or wrong have no place in the fast-paced lives of Kusturica's protagonists. Their behaviour is nothing but a reaction to the social environment. Faith is rejected, as it does not succeed in supplying the criteria for morality. In line with what can be described as a Marxist-influenced view, morality is seen as socially and not transcendentally conditioned.

History/Memory

> As a matter of principle, I do not like political films, I prefer that the historical events serve as a background to other situations.
>
> 1985 interview, quoted in Bertellini, 1995, p. 27

Even when he paints a panoramic picture developing over decades, as in *Underground*, and even when his protagonists cross paths with the whims of history, as in *Father*, Kusturica brings it all down to the individual. All we can know about social process is played out in this individual's experience. Thus, the specific construction of historiographical narratives in Kusturica's films is informed by a positivist approach: the only valid

knowledge is the knowledge that is acquired in our immediate practice;
anything beyond is speculation.

Kusturica's aversion to epic narratives, which may be informing his positivist attitude to history, is clearly seen in *Father*. In this film he approaches
the relationship of individual and history not as a historical fresco but as a
'historical love film' where the epic is substituted for an intimate story limited to a single family, the basic unit of the director's social universe.
Discussing *Father* he said:

> [My film] does not want to analyse History, but to talk of the crisis of the man
> caught in a moment of our contemporary history. It analyses a family like a
> model of the architecture of human life; and this model resists and persists,
> happily, all the attacks of history and politics.
>
> *Libération*, 17 October 1995, quoted in 'Papa est ...', p. 77

And elsewhere:

> I was only trying to make a film that was capable of showing the way history
> created pressure on people. The historical process is best described from
> the perspective of someone who is not involved in the creation of history –
> someone who is just affected by it. Because a person like that is capable of
> suffering from historical circumstances.
>
> Kusturica, quoted in Attanasio, 1985, p. C1

No wonder, then, that in Kusturica's films the agents of history are usually
individual members of the small face-to-face community (extended family,
neighbourhood), who act as intermediaries of the historical and social
processes (Ankica in *Father*, Marko in *Underground*). In *Father*, for example,
it is the regime that ultimately imprisons Meša. But that would not happen
were it not for the intrigue of his mistress and brother-in-law, who accidentally have access to the social mechanisms that allow them to play a dirty
trick on him, thus functioning as intermediaries of the higher social forces
at work here. Similarly, while the topic of *Underground* may be social
processes and history, the only real 'agent' here is Marko who, once again,
functions as an intermediary of higher forces. If people end up in the cellar,
it is not only because a war is raging outside, but also because Marko, one of

them, has decided to use them as slave labour, having betrayed them within the immediate community. In such a context, the ups and downs of history are seen as peripeteia in the neighbourhood, and its agents as double-dealing swindlers who seek either to take revenge (Ankica) or to betray (Marko). It would seem that the historical process is brought into the narrative mostly to allow the director to show how some 'local heroes', operating from within the community, take advantage of historical circumstances and trick others for their own ends.

Once the ordinary members of the community come to reflect on adverse experiences in the aftermath they blame it all on some inscrutable external power that coerced those relatives or neighbours to act nasty. Even though they confront the concrete perpetrators, they tend to explain trouble within the community by the workings of unintelligible forces that have set 'brother against brother' and are beyond their control. The duress may have been brought about by the actions of the 'brother' who took up the role of agent of history, but it is the sweeping social turmoil at large that is ultimately identified as the reason for hardship. Thus, by ascribing it all to some unfathomable superior will, the victims effectively absolve the perpetrators; they can all go on living next door to each other, enjoying wedding celebrations together, oblivious to the past.

That the perpetrators of evil and adverse experiences are clearly people from the immediate environment who acted of their own free will makes it impossible to ultimately indict a given social order or even concrete historical personages. This is seen in the treatment of Tito, for example. Even though Kusturica has asserted repeatedly that he holds Tito personally responsible for many of the problems of contemporary Yugoslavia, in *Underground* Tito never becomes a fully fledged agent of history. At the end of the 'Cold War' part of the film, set in 1961, Marko runs away from the scene, not to re-surface for more than thirty years – 1992, twelve years after Tito's death. But what happens with Tito (and Titoism respectively) after Marko's escape? How are the twenty years between Marko's exit and Tito's death handled in the film? An intertitle informs the viewers that Marko's disappearance saddened comrade Tito so much that he fell ill, stayed ill for the next twenty years and finally died (in 1980).

It is a curious narrative device, where, as Hutcheon remarks, 'the real figures of the past are deployed to validate or authenticate the fictional world by their presence' (1988, p. 114). The years between 1961 and 1980 were a very important period for Tito's Yugoslavia and many of the problems that led to the country's break-up can be traced back to Tito's policies at this time. But Kusturica has no way to keep Tito in the frame. Because Marko, the fictional agent of history, has disappeared, the real agent of history, Tito, has got to disappear from the narrative as well. In Kusturica's view of history it is not possible to keep someone like Tito as an agent of what happens to the people in the film for the simple reason that he is not one of the small community that is the basic element of his narrative universe.

As far as memory is concerned, Kusturica clearly favours the individual over the public record. During the wedding scene near the end of *Father*, Meša tells Zijo that he can forget what happened to him, but he cannot forgive it. This sentence is repeated during the wedding scene at the end of *Underground*, only in reverse order: Blacky tells Marko that he can forgive but cannot forget. It is a reversal that gives the individual mode of remembrance a superior standing in relation to any public version of history. History is what the protagonists experienced and will be remembered in their own emotive way.

By supplying personal memory with such privileged status, Kusturica treats history in much the same way as it is treated in *Forrest Gump* (directed by Robert Zemeckis), yet another hugely successful film which swept the Oscars just months before *Underground* premiered at Cannes. In analysing Zemeckis' film, Robert Burgoyne spoke of 'prosthetic memory', a concept that seems to be particularly suitable in exploring Kusturica's take on Yugoslav history as well. According to Burgoyne, the narrative strategy in *Forrest Gump* was expressed in the 'effort to disengage cultural memory from public history', thus creating 'subjective connections to the national past', and, in this way, calling forth the sense of 'I' and 'we' that makes the national narrative compelling and meaningful.

> In severing history – understood as the register of public events outside the spectrum of individual experience – from what it envisions as the authentic texture of national life, the film creates a kind of prosthetic memory of the

period, refunctioning the cultural memory of the sixties so that it can be integrated into the traditional narrative of nation. It thus imagines America as a kind of virtual nation whose historical debts have been forgiven and whose disabilities have all been corrected.

Kusturica, quoted in Burgoyne, 1997, pp. 14–15

In a similar way, in *Underground* Kusturica severed the highly fictionalised narrative of what he considered the authentic texture of national life from history ('understood as the register of public events outside the spectrum of individual experience'). Going back as far as the time of World War II and the early 1960s, he 'refunctioned' the public record of Yugoslav history by replacing it with vernacular popular opinion of the roles of the various nationalities and forces in the nation's dissolution. He exposed the communist tampering with memory but replaced it with selective use of documentary footage pointing at the Slovenes and the Croats as Nazi sympathisers, in a film that was meant to subvert the very process of the construction of 'facts' in historical narratives. He mocked the non-aligned movement by using extended documentary footage from Tito's funeral, a curious event that in 1980 brought together a whole range of incompatible international politicians (from Nikolae Ceausescu and King Hussein of Jordan to Margaret Thatcher and Leonid Brezhnev), thus making a point about the pragmatism of all Cold War politics and ideology. He showed a busy network of underground tunnels running under Europe and linking Athens to Berlin in 1961, thus suggesting that political divisions and stagnation were public relations hypocrisy that was effectively cancelled by the lively clandestine traffic of vernacular migrations. He featured Yugoslav arms dealers in continuous cordial relations with both Russian and German counterparts at a time when these were supposed to be enemies, thus indicating that the profits of the arms trade were the sole thing that mattered for these formal ideological opponents. And, most importantly, he wrapped it all up with the memorably nostalgic image of the Danube wedding, where all the adversaries come resolutely together, no matter what. In all this, to transpose Burgoyne's *Forrest Gump* observations onto *Underground*, Kusturica constructed a 'prosthetic memory' of his homeland. He created a vision in which the 'true' Yugoslavia was re-imagined as a kind of virtual nation whose unhappy fate was corrected and historical debts cancelled, albeit momentarily, in a single gesture of forgiveness (if not forgetting) in the sunshine of the final wedding scene.

Drawing on the thoughts of post-modern theorists – Linda Hutcheon's views on historiographic metafictions (1988, pp. 105–23) and Robert Rosenstone's discussion of post-modern history writing and film (1998, p. 206) – Igor Krstic compiled a list of criteria for post-modernist historiographical film-making that particularly apply to Kusturica (1999, p. 145), which I use here in a modified version:

1. Self-reflexive narration: continuous referencing to the constructed nature of narratives and to the fictional nature of film itself. Privileging narration that evolves around the notion of subjectivity while simultaneously incapable of finding a subject in which he/she is confident of his/her ability to know the past with any certainty, thus problematising the very act of inscribing subjectivity into history. Extensive use of intertextual referencing.

2. Refusal to take storytelling seriously. Using parody and irony in order to reveal the constructed nature of normative representations like realism. Approaching the past with humour – absurdist, surrealist, dadaesque attitudes.

3. Blurring traditional boundaries and subverting hierarchical categories and oppositions, like fact and fiction, truth and imagination or good and evil and combining mutually exclusive genres like documentary with melodrama and satire, *film noir* with slapstick or fantasy. Altering and inventing incidents and characters.

4. Questioning interpretative conventions. Consciousness of history as a constructed narrative and interest in meta-narrative. Representing historical events from a non-traditional and often subjective point of view. Accepting, even glorifying one's own selectivity, cultural bias, partialism, partisanship and rhetorical approach. Refusal to focus or to sum up the meaning of past events, but making sense of them in a partial and open-ended, rather than totalised, manner. Rejection of the sense of cultural universality.

In his post-modernist approach to Yugoslavia's past, Kusturica subverted the official historiographic practice that operates with 'facts' and 'meaning' as constituents of an 'event'. In *Underground* he mocked the communist historical epics glorifying the resistance fighters and Tito and showed how communism grossly tampered with historical memory. The wheeler-dealer affairs of the protagonists during the war are later beautified in a heroic light and overblown in significance. Incidents of drunken womanising are represented as heroic deeds in Marko's memoirs written for the sole purpose of serving the needs of communist myth-making. Kusturica unmasks this overzealous 'production of history' in the subplot that evolves around the grotesque scenes from the set of *Spring Comes on a White Horse*, meant to expose the practices of official Yugoslav historiography.

In his effort to show the subtler aspects of an individual's coping with difficult moments brought about by social events, however, Kusturica approaches social change as something inherently adverse that needs to be taken as it comes, to be endured. Writing in *Le Monde* in 1985, the leading Yugoslav writer Danilo Kiš criticised *Father*'s vision of history as 'cruel': Kusturica's world, Kiš claimed, did not include revolt as a possible scenario. Conscious of their own insignificance, all the protagonists care about is to somehow survive the blows of fate, the way they would do their best to survive a natural catastrophe. Their behaviour was marked by a 'certain oriental fatalism, where the blows not only remain unanswered but are taken without reproach and without objection' (17 October 1985, in 'Papa est ...', p. 74).

It may well be that this comment provides a key to Kusturica's understanding of the relationship of individual and history: all people can do in response to the assault of history is to hold on somehow, to shelter themselves, be it by becoming conformists (like Meša in *Father*) or by entering a cocoon (like the cellar inhabitants in *Underground*). It is a vision of history that does not leave space for excitement, for participation by one's own free will.

Communism

In general, class is not a concept that Kusturica works with, he prefers the smaller unit of face-to-face community. He is not really interested in the hardships faced by the Roma, and their class concerns are not a focal point of his Gypsy films. His *Arizona* sidesteps issues of class or other social inequality. Thus, communism and the specific limitations it imposes on the individual are the only social concerns that have ever been seriously addressed by Kusturica, who makes communism a subject of exploration in three films: in *Dolly Bell* communism is domesticated and tackled with a smile; in *Father* it raises some more serious concerns; in *Underground* it is indicted for ruining a country and a generation.

If considered in the context of East European film-making of the time, it is no wonder that the treatment of communism is at the centre of Kusturica's interest during the first half of the 1980s. This was when the whole region's cinema came to critically dissect the repercussions of communism on personal lives, as seen in seminal films like Wajda's *Man of Marble*, Pál Gábor's *Angi Vera* (1979), Márta Mészáros's *Napló gyermekeimnek* (*Diary for My Children*, 1982), Rajko Grlić's *You Only Love Once*, Janusz Zaorski's *Matka Królów* (*Mother of Kings*, 1982) and many others. Within Yugoslav cinema itself, the difficult years of the split with Stalin were in the sphere of interest of many film-makers. One of the most important films of that era – Stole Popov's *Srecna Nova '49* (*Happy New '49*, 1986), scripted by Gordan Mihić and set in the Macedonian capital of Skopje – shares a sensibility very similar to *Father*.

The socio-political context in which *Underground* was made seems radically different: after the end of the communist system, after the fall of the Berlin Wall and after the demise of the Soviet Union. But even at this time, communism remained of central interest for Kusturica. Responding to ongoing concerns over the deep political crisis in Yugoslavia, the majority of 1995 critical interpretations of *Underground* concentrated on the film's take on nationalism, thus overlooking the fact that it was as much a reaction to the legacy of communism as it was to the break-up of Yugoslavia. While the chunk of land floating away was a metaphor for an irretrievably fragmented Yugoslavia, the cellar was a metaphor for communism and it worked powerfully. Not ethnic strife but rather the twisted nature of communism was the focus of attention for most of the film. The very dedication ('to our fathers and their children', i.e. 'to ourselves') clearly suggested that the film was addressed to those who had lived in communist Yugoslavia and experienced its downfall.

The film, however, did not really explore this generation's experiences with communism, since the thirty-year period between 1961 to 1992 that roughly coincided with the formative years of 'the children' was effectively scrapped from the narrative. Didn't this decision in structuring historical time reflect the view that the generation of 'the fathers' was responsible for everything that happened? Wasn't the choice to black out the thirty-year period of 'mature socialism' an indirect refusal to admit that the generation of 'the children' also had something to do with the failure of Yugoslavia?

The Yugoslav brand of state socialism had not been as harsh as the tyrannical Russian version. But even when associated with Tito's white uniform and showy lifestyle, it was still a system built on sectarianism and indoctrination. Having had the chance to observe the way ordinary Communist Party members thought and acted, Kusturica had the advantage over his Western counterparts who attempted to make films about communists. Reiterating that the only good thing about communism were its mistakes, he was nonetheless more understanding because he could follow the logic of those communist-believers who were not necessarily fanatics or leaders. Kusturica knew communism's confines and painted its contradictions humorously, particularly the discrepancy between its twisted rhetoric and the reality that failed to live up to its five-year plans. Most of all, he was interested in communism as it interfered with the patriarchal set-up in domestic power relations.

The relationship between Dino and his dying father in *Dolly Bell* emphasised the existential dimensions of loss and coming of age, but played out through an ongoing dispute over the essence of the perfect society, in which father and son represented two divergent ideological lines. The father used familiar agitprop clichés to paint a picture of a flawless harmonious utopia where everyone 'will receive according to their needs', and 'will contribute according to their abilities'. Dino opposed him with 'individualist-humanist' ideas that, at the time, represented the essential critique of communist ideology – that for society to grow, the individual must come to perfection first.

But this film's main concern was not to sort out communism's rights and wrongs. *Dolly Bell*'s achievement was much more in presenting the comical interplay of conflicting opinions and the adjustments that ideology was compelled to undergo within the domestic sphere. The real problem with the views of the father was not that they were flawed, but that they revealed his conformity. Even though he talked of authentic Marxism and claimed possession of several volumes of Marx's writings, he actually exposed himself by reciting propaganda lines from the omnipresent agitprop brochures. Dino was also indoctrinated, but at least he took his opinions from a clandestine book on hypnosis. He did not really oppose the communist ideal – if he had, it would have meant open confrontation with the father, a rebellion against patriarchy. All he wanted to do was negotiate the terms of own filial succession within patriarchy by creating a situation where his mildly dissenting views were tolerated.

Father was a specific indictment of 1950s state socialism – for keeping people trapped and for disturbing the basic family balance. But, as if reiterating the Gramscian view that oppressive power relations are maintained by consent, the father (the affected protagonist) was prepared to stay trapped and be part of the game. After his release from the camp he did not become a secluded dissident but once again rushed back to climbing the social ladder. While at the beginning of the film he still retained some free judgment, later he was effectively re-educated and learned to keep his opinions (if any) to himself. Not only was he eager to be restored to his former position, he never swore at the authorities or questioned communism, turning into a perfect malleable individual. He was, indeed, coerced into being a conformist. But he was an opportunist, too.

As in *Dolly Bell*, in *Father* the critical questioning of communism came from the younger generation, in this case Malik. He realised that his friend's father had committed suicide in some faraway camp and that the adults had buried an empty coffin. He knew that the place of his father's 'business trip' was a penal colony. He understood why the neighbour says it is only 'safe' to sing Mexican songs. The fact that it was delivered by a child, however, meant that this criticism became no more than mischievous mockery.

Once the ordeal of imprisonment and internment was over, it transpired that it all came down to male rivalry over a female; the scrutiny of communism as an inhuman social system was effectively cancelled. All ideology came down, once again, to domestic power struggles. Communism was implicated only so far as it supplied the extra political means in the struggle of the rivals' mating game. The imprisonment happened because of a personal betrayal and its repercussions were shown through the effect it had on the family, the primary patriarchal world of Kusturica's interest. At the end, however, the family was happily together; the basic unit of society was repaired. The scars were not too deep and people's lives were not damaged profoundly. Like *Dolly Bell*, *Father* was more about the restoration of patriarchal balance rather than about the wounds inflicted by communism.

A decade later, *Underground* revisited a similar combination of communism and opportunism. Once again the conceptualisation of social process was structured along the lines of a mating game (Marko and Blacky's competition over Natalija) that played out against the backdrop of a neighbourhood setting (the cellar) inhabited by members of an extended family who willingly maintained the patriarchal balance by worshipping Marko as a 'saviour'. While in Kusturica's earlier work, the attention had been on the simple people that communism manipulated and abused, the subject of *Underground* was the manipulator, the perpetrator whose amorality is beyond any political system. Marko enslaved a group of people, appropriating their lives for decades by playing their saviour while in fact acting as their master in the cellar where he was keeping them in 'hiding'. But the exact motives for Marko's exploitation affair never became clear. He did not seem to be really connected to any social movement and his declared involvement with communism, once again, was a purely opportunistic one. He was involved in shady dealings with whoever happened to be in power at the time, but his manipulation was not a logical extension of the flaws of state socialism. Rather, it all happened because Marko lived in a Balkan world where swindlers like him are the only reliable entrepreneurs and where social and economic dynamics are the consequence of the power mechanics of the neighbourhood.

All the communists in Kusturica are, in fact, opportunists of a specifically Balkan kind. They are communists just because communism happens to be there, but they are not committed to it in any conscious way; they are simply using it as a vehicle for petty individualist objectives. They can play by the rules if needed, as do Mustafa in *Dolly Bell* and Meša in *Father*. But they also have the energy to discard the rules, as Marko and Blacky do in *Underground*, to keep themselves on top of volatile fortune. They may act in the name of ideology but their actions are determined by clearly definable (and usually small-scale) pragmatic goals. The communist system provided a nourishing environment for such untidy Balkan personalities. Like many real-life communist leaders, Marko was a deceiver and did not care a toss for communist ideals; to him it was not about deceit, but about husky survivalism. Even Blacky, the simpleton, who was shown as a devoted follower of Tito, was more of a black marketeer, a Balkan individualist with no need of ideologies and authorities. No wonder that he was the one who turned nationalist warrior and destroyer, fighting not for a country but solely for himself, as seen in *Underground*'s final part.

The Great Powers

In the past, the balance in the Balkans was defined by the Ottoman Empire and Austria-Hungary. Later on, Yugoslavia's fate was mostly influenced by what were known as the Big Powers in the West (mostly Germany and later the USA) and the East (the Soviet Union and later Russia). Kusturica has regularly expressed his opinion on the effect of the Big Powers' continuous impact on the history of the region.

To him Germany is an essentially Nazi state; in the past it backed the genocidal Ustasha regime and in the 1990s it hastened Yugoslavia's break-up by encouraging Croatia's rushed secession. Every war in Yugoslavia, Kusturica noted, has something to do with Austrians and Germans, and he talked of his 'disgust' for Germans (1993, p. 35).

These views on Germany were developed in *Underground*. In the film's longer version today's Germans are represented as racists still fascinated with the ideas of Arian superiority, eugenics and phrenology: a view illustrated by the extended scene where a racist German professor demonstrates the 'Balkan subject' Ivan to medical students.

Russia is also an adverse foreign power; its defeat in a football match is a cause for celebration in *Father*. Unlike Germany, however, it is a

Slavic country and therefore the Russians and Russia are not really resented. Like some of his father's friends (who were imprisoned for being Soviet sympathisers), Kusturica's protagonists in *Underground* love Russia. They frequent a pub called 'Mala Moskva' ('Little Moscow'), make references to Russian art and literature and hope that the Soviets will win the war.

Though only occasional images of post-communist Russians have so far appeared in his films (e.g. the smugglers of the 'Maxim Gorky' in *Black Cat*), the director has underlined his interest in the new Russian migrations since the early 1990s. In interviews he has repeatedly talked of his fascination with the new Russian diaspora, with the Russian mafia and with Russian kitsch. His unrealised *Crime and Punishment* and the new project called *The Nose* are both set among Russians in America.

But then, unlike most other communist countries, no occupying Soviet forces were ever stationed on Yugoslav territory, so Kusturica has not lived the experiences that inform the anti-Russian sentiments of other East European film-makers. He is clear that small nations are doomed to depend on imperial powers, but he is proud to belong to 'pagan and rebellious Yugoslavia', a country which even though little was 'big enough to eat its own shit while the Czechs, Slovaks and Bulgarians were forced to eat Russian shit' (1993, p. 28). When it comes to dependency, Russia seems to be the preferred choice: a Soviet sympathiser in *Father* is quoted as saying: 'I would rather eat Russian shit than American cake!'

The West in general does not enjoy very favourable standing with Kusturica. He never misses a chance to express his contempt for American television, which he believes has routinely misrepresented the essence of the Yugoslav conflict. The West has been an adversary before – the Nazis bombed Belgrade, but so too did the Allied forces and both bombings are shown and commented on in *Underground*. In this context Kusturica was, logically, an outspoken opponent of the NATO bombing of Serbia over Kosovo in 1999 and gave many angry interviews condemning the aggression.

In *Black Cat* he represented the West in the phantom image of a river liner that passes by on the Danube – men in tuxedoes and women in evening dresses waltz on the upper deck, oblivious of the Yugoslav Gypsies who watch them from the shore.

Yugoslavism

Kusturica liked the multi-culturalism and the diversity of Yugoslavia and would have preferred the country to stay together. He was a product of Yugoslavia, as it were, and his situation as a Bosnian cinematic *wunderkind* had been particularly advantageous. He would probably not have stayed in Yugoslavia even if the country had remained at peace, but he was genuinely unhappy about the hostilities that came about. During the conflict, he was overtaken by a feeling of deprivation, of strong disillusionment over the loss of his Yugoslav 'imagined community'. After Tito's death all the mockery of democratic institutions became apparent and a political vacuum was established, Kusturica said (*South Bank Show* documentary, 2000). The events that followed were interpreted as a story of betrayal, along the lines of Kusturica's favoured narrative framework: Yugoslavia failed because it was destroyed from within. The Slovene and the Croats betrayed the Union for their own petty interests, to become once again the independent (but in fact marionette) states that they had been in the past.

In 1993 Kusturica admitted that he had tended to neglect what was happening in Yugoslavia in the late 1980s. Due to his profession, he had become impervious to certain things, a little bit cocooned. But later he felt the need to get involved again with what he still believed was his country (Bouineau, 1993, p. 67).

The most systematic account of Kusturica's views on Yugoslavia is found in a 1993 confessional essay called *Une profession de foi (A Profession of Faith)*, written by the director in Serbo-Croatian and translated into French. This twenty-page text appears in Bouineau's book (pp. 16–37) and is representative of Kusturica's mind-set on Yugoslav issues at the time when he was preparing to make *Underground*. Here, Kusturica asks himself what happened to his romantic dream of Yugoslavia. He speaks openly about his suffering over his nation's demise, a painful experience affecting all the members of his generation. He cannot discuss Yugoslavia except in personal terms – as a 'personal drama' (p. 36) over the loss of a 'romantic dream' (p. 29), as an intimate experience of coming of age, where maturity comes along with disillusionment.

> The idea of fatherland and patriotism for me was not connected to a nation but to my garden in front of the one-bedroom flat where I lived with my parents; fatherland was this garden, my garden and the pals whom I only knew by first names and with whom I exchanged pictures of the Yugoslav national football players.
>
> 1993, p. 18

The fragrance of the acacia that blossomed in front of his window is the strongest memory of this feeling of belonging (p. 18). Back then he believed in Yugoslav unity, and thought his patriotic feelings as a Bosnian-Yugoslav boy were more or less identical with the feelings of everybody else across Yugoslavia: that they too 'cried with happiness when we beat the Krauts (even if it happened rarely)' and were equally proud when 'the flag of my little country' was raised at the Olympic games (p. 18). But he soon realised he was wrong. As soon as he grew up and his first successes came, people from the Western republics of Yugoslavia became envious of him and came to hate him, 'endlessly' (p. 20). They could not accept the fact that someone from a place as 'primitive' as Bosnia, which they called by the derogatory name 'Katanga', would 'receive the top award at the world's biggest festival, while those in Ljubljana, of whom Hitler's *Mein Kampf* said they had developed an authentic national culture, did not even figure in the official selection' (p. 20).

In the past, there had been a specific brand of Yugoslav communism which he calls 'monarcho-bolshevism' (p. 18). The country was a state ruled by two men – Tito (a Croat) and his main economic adviser, Edvard Kardelj (a Slovenian) (p. 20). Their incompetent social engineering and their nations' superficial commitment to the ideal of Yugoslav supranationalism was, according to Kusturica, accountable for most of Yugoslavia's troubles.

To Kusturica, the Slovenes had acted historically as 'Austrian grooms' (p. 20) and Nazi sympathisers. They were hypocritical in their commitment to Yugoslavia, so it was no wonder they led the drive to leave the union at the first signs of duress (p. 20). They were responsible for starting the war because they felt they were losing their privileged economic standing

(p. 36). The Croats were faithful Nazi allies during World War II and carried out genocide against Serbs and other ethnic groups (p. 24). But for the sake of reconciliation and in the name of Yugoslav supranationalism, in postwar Yugoslavia the Croat Ustasha genocidal crimes were banned from public discourse and never properly addressed (p. 24), thus important historical wounds were never allowed to heal. Even more, historical truth was misrepresented, mostly in two aspects: the Croats washed their hands by blaming indigenous Ustasha crimes on the Nazis; on top of this, they claimed to have been the backbone of the anti-fascist movement, while it was a known fact that most of the partisans were Serbs (p. 36). Today, Croat nationalists wanted to play their old games of eyeball gouging and finger chopping (p. 36) all over again.

Within Yugoslavia, Bosnians were always kept on the margins. Kusturica quotes the writer Meša Selimović, who described the Muslims as a community that was not big enough to become a lake, but not small enough to remain a pond (p. 32). This is why both Croats and Serbs had claims over them (p. 26). And this is why, though the epicentre of the earthquake may not have been in their immediate vicinity, its tremors were felt most strongly in Bosnia (p. 35). The Bosnian Muslim community is secular and pagan in its essence; Kusturica is particularly disapproving of the recent Islamist trend. To him Bosnian Muslim nationalism is as dangerous as the other nationalisms that emerged in Yugoslavia's break-up (p. 35); on other occasions he repeatedly asserts that it has effectively led to the destruction of the rich Bosnian cultural legacy. 'To have gone through such hell, these guys have done nothing to shake the world. They don't have good movies, good books, good dramas – nothing. That proves there is something fake in it. Ideology is above everything else there,' Kusturica said of the Bosnians (Feinstein, 1999, p. 7).

The Serbs, in contrast, are a 'credulous' and 'hedonist' people with an 'emotional comprehension of justice', which is why they get involved in war so easily (1993, p. 31). They fought against fascism in World War II, and Bosnian Muslims like Kusturica's father fought alongside (p. 24). Serbia was the least nationalistic republic, but while all other brands of nationalism – Croat, Slovene and Bosnian – were deemed legitimate, the Serbs were never allowed to be openly nationalistic (1993, p. 21). Even though the Serbs were deemed privileged, in fact they were at a disadvantage. Within Yugoslavia, they were never ruled by one of their own; they always had to be considerate and yield to the other nationalities, thus leaving their own people in political deprivation (p. 22). Unlike the Croats and the Slovenes, however, the Serbs failed to explain themselves to the world at the time of the conflict, even though their position was historically and morally superior (p. 31).

*   *   *

Underground, and particularly the long version of the film, reflected these views. In the film he tried to bring to light the unrecognised historical responsibilities of the nations that constituted Yugoslavia for the country's break-up. Treating history through the prism of community politics, he exposed the betrayal within the extended family of Yugoslav nations. The extended version of the film, however, confirmed what Pavle Levi called the film's 'all too easy identification of entire ethnic groups with the genocidal policies of the Ustashas and their supporters' (2001, p. 10). In his intention to mercilessly expose, Kusturica ended up laying charges of collective guilt.

Even though he had tried to remain truthful, by 1993 Kusturica realised that it was not possible to be objective any longer (1993, p. 23). With *Underground*, he said, he lost his 'political innocence' (Bertellini, 1996, p. 19).

'Every time I try to help Yugoslavia, I think of it as if it is one people and this is what I have been mistaken about' Kusturica said (1993, p. 36). By the mid-1990s the director knew this had been a naïve and childish belief. The Yugoslavs were not one people and not a united football team, as he used to think in his parent's apartment with the fragrant acacia at the window. Kusturica was angry with all those who deceived him by not being as faithful to the Yugoslav idea as he was. What made him most angry, however, was that with their disloyal acts they had taken away his adolescent illusion of belonging and had forced him into maturity. It was this forced growing up, this continuous suffering over a demolished childhood identity, that was the key to understanding the director's personal involvement with Yugoslavia's disintegration. His statements referred to politics, history and nationalism,

but to him it all came down to the categories of his own narrative universe
structured around the tribulations of coming of age.

Public and private

> For me, the family possesses a mythical dimension in which you could easily
> insert the drama. The family is the core of drama.
>
> Kusturica, quoted in Bouineau, 1993, p. 71

Ordinary and often traditional nuclear and extended families, sticking
together in happy and troubled times, take a central place in the director's
narratives, from *Dolly Bell* and *Father* to *Black Cat*. The only 'dysfunctional'
family – Grace and Elaine's in *Arizona* – is an American one; but it is
counter-balanced by the image of a happy, traditional and supportive family seen in the home movie footage of Axel's childhood.

It all begins and ends with the family and the immediate community. To
make sense of the other dimensions in Kusturica's social world one needs to
refer back to these basic units of society. The community in Kusturica is a
small one where people, neighbours and relatives, know each other and are
involved in daily face-to-face interactions. The protagonist moves among
extended family members and friends (*kumove**) who may also be business
associates. Besides relatives, the community also comprises neighbourhood
friends that Dino hangs out with (*Dolly Bell*), Malik's neighbours (*Father*),
Perhan's neighbours and local gangsters transposed to Italy (*Gypsies*),
friends (*Arizona*), *kumove* and friends (*Underground*) and the Romani neighbourhood (*Black Cat*).

It is usually someone from within the immediate community who sets
the story in motion by undertaking moves to betray the others. A driving
force of the action, at least one betrayal occurs in each film and sometimes
more. In *Father*, Meša is betrayed by his mistress and brother-in-law.
Ultimately, it is his womanising and not his political loyalties that brings all

---

* The institution of *kumstvo*, even though not based on blood relationship, is a key feature of the
extended family structure in the Balkans, with the *kum* (best man at the wedding of the family)
enjoying a special trusted status as a family's guardian.

When Father Was Away on Business: Sena's taking a place next to Zijo is also a form of revenge

his troubles about. But it is not about Meša's questionable political views. Politics are just an extra weapon in the range of means available within the power dynamics of the domestic sphere. In *Gypsies*, Perhan is betrayed by Ahmed; in *Underground* everyone is betrayed by Marko. All events in *Black Cat* revolve around betrayals: Matko is betrayed in every business venture, to survive he needs to lie, he betrays his own son by agreeing to marry him off to Dadan's midget sister, Ida's grandmother betrays her by trying to get her engaged to Dadan, and Afrodita betrays the wedding by escaping.

Then, there is the revenge that comes in response to the betrayal. It does not always take the form of an open confrontation (as in *Gypsies*, where Perhan kills Ahmed and is killed in revenge soon thereafter). By raping Ankica in the basement, Meša takes revenge not only on her but also on his brother-in-law. Even more, his insistence that Sena make up with Zijo is also a form of revenge, an assertion of moral superiority. He does not need to take revenge on the unjust social order that imprisoned him; it is sufficient (and more important) to take vengeance on the relative who acted treacherously.

In these narratives, public and private are constructed as mutually exclusive and inherently antagonistic spheres. As in the opposition of above and below, events that take place in public are linked to appearances, while those of the private sphere are seen as essence. The public sphere is effectively lessened and diminished in favour of the private one. In *Father*, Malik and his father repeatedly rehearse a patriotic speech that the boy is to deliver at a pioneer event. When the crucial moment comes, however, Malik forgets the exact wording of praise for the Communist Party and Tito, thus putting his father's political trustworthiness in jeopardy. Malik experiences his failure to perform, literally and symbolically, as a disaster. The father attempts to comfort him, but in fact sends mixed signals: why did the boy need to go through all the trouble rehearsing the speech to be told at the end that it does not really matter, it is all a show? In this scene of paternal reassurance, father and son form a bond. Public life is equated with the theatre and the family circle is established as the little private haven where one does not need to perform, to put on a show.

Life in public means to 'perform' most of the time. The Romani children in *Gypsies* are taught how to 'perform' as beggars. In *Arizona* Paul Leger, Axel's friend, performs scenes from well-known movies and even claims that his name means 'born to play' in French. But it is the Cadillac dealership where he has to perform the most to fascinate the clients. It is his abhorrence of such performing in public that keeps Axel away from the idea of becoming a salesman. Marko in *Underground* is unsympathetic precisely because he has accepted performing in public as a natural mode of life, has forsaken the private and has betrayed his face-to-face community and family.

The family may be seen as a mainstay of patriarchy by some, but to Kusturica it is a genuinely sheltering place. The domestic space is positioned as the only sphere of genuine feelings and actions. Patriarchy does not seem to bother the director. He even paints it in a positive light, particularly in the Sarajevo films (see Horton, 1998). A family with an absent father, for example, is a family with a disturbed balance – the loss of the father in *Dolly Bell* leads to an unwanted accelerated maturity; the need to restore the patriarchal balance is the driving force of narrative in *Father*. On some occasions – in *Brides* and in *Gypsies* – classical patriarchy is substituted by matriarchy. Sometimes a member of the extended family, like Uncle Leo in *Arizona*, takes on the patriarchal function. The crime lord, Ahmed, fills the hierarchical void of Perhan's missing parents and grandmother. People in *Underground* want to be led and are fully content to be sheltered in the cellar of patriarchal guidance. The patriarchs in *Black Cat* are the nicest and liveliest people around; families are incomplete without them, so no wonder the director's choice is to bring them back to life.

In contrast to narratives where the defeat of patriarchal structures is made a precondition for the liberation of the protagonist, in Kusturica the tendency is towards restoration of a disturbed patriarchal order. Patriarchy is not something bad that has to be destroyed for the sake of self-assertion. On the contrary – clear hierarchies within the immediate neighbourhood, the domestic sphere and the extended family are a precondition for the refuge that the individual needs. Patriarchy is the sheltering environment that protects the protagonist from maturity, that keeps him in the blissful stage of adolescence and indefinitely postpones the dreaded moment of coming of age.

Rites of passage

Kusturica's interest lies much more with the everyday than with the epic, with the individual than the collective. It is the individual's experiences that concern him more than what is happening with society or which way history is going. He does not really want to make historical films because of the intricacy of the underlying politics and because in his view history comes down to an individual's experience. If it were not for his Yugoslav roots which compel him to work with historical material, his films would probably feature stories of coming of age exclusively, like Perhan's and Axel's. But even now, most of Kusturica's films are about coming of age, revolving around the life-cycle categories of lost innocence and imposed maturity.

Like Tarkovsky and Fellini's films, where 'the protagonists are people who never become men but always remain children' (Boni, 1999, p. 24), Kusturica prefers heroes who occupy a subtle space in-between, suspended between adolescence and adulthood. Like other European directors, he is inclined to see the early years as the source for soul-searching inspiration and as a key to understanding the way things are experienced in adult life. 'If all Europe keeps persistently returning to the ancient Greeks, why wouldn't I keep returning to my childhood?' he said (quoted in Boni, 1999, p. 39).

Children are present throughout his films – the little brother and sister in *Dolly Bell*, Perhan's sister and son in *Gypsies* and the children running around the wedding table in *Underground*. But apart from *Father*, their presence is not particularly prominent or central. It is not childhood that ultimately excites him; he is much more preoccupied with the next period in the life cycle.

This interest in adolescence informs Kusturica's film-making. It is not exclusive to him, of course: adolescence has been a prevailing interest for writers and film-makers of all generations; it was at the centre of a whole literary genre (*Bildungsroman*) and it has been the informative point of numerous cinematic works. But while directors like Truffaut, who also look into the childhood and the adolescent years of their alter ego protagonists (Antoine Doinel), revisit their subject later in his adult life, Kusturica does not seem to be interested in exploring things beyond a certain point. His narratives either end at the moment when the protagonist reaches maturity (Dino, Axel), or with the death of the protagonist who has grown up (Perhan).

The process of coming of age revolves around several variables. First of all, there is the gradual change in appearance and the acceptance of the new body shape and looks. Bland-looking at first, Dino ends up as a handsome boy. The bespectacled and shabby Perhan evolves into a self-confident and good-looking young man. (Axel's appearance does not change so much and he remains equally good looking throughout most of *Arizona*, but this probably has more to do with Johnny Depp's star persona than with Kusturica's artistic vision.) Then, there is the discovery of sex –

in a pigeon shack (*Dolly Bell*), in a paddleboat (*Gypsies*), or in a sunflower field (*Black Cat*) – as something magnificent and very pure. Sexual initiation is a great defining experience and none of the protagonists grows disillusioned about it. On the contrary, it becomes a source of inspiration for each one of them.

Another dimension is overcoming dependency on the previous generation. It is played out in Dino's sad and friendly parting with his ailing father, in Malik's empowering distrust of his father as a role model, in Perhan's departure from his grandmother and in Axel's farewell with the dying Uncle Leo. In general, the parting with those in a position of authority has sad overtones; it does not usually happen in open confrontation and does not lead to the destruction of entrenched hierarchies. (An exception is seen in the case of Marko's brother in *Underground*, Ivan, who takes over fifty years to mature. He has to destroy Marko by the very logic of emancipation from his monstrous sibling.)

Yet another aspect of coming of age is gradual socialisation, the finding of one's own place in the world. The protagonists have little control over these things and depend largely on the circumstances. Dino probably does not have a very clear image of himself as a guitar player in a rock band, but others have made the choice for him already. Perhan does not intend to be a gangster, but is coerced into becoming one. Axel keeps resisting Leo's plan to make him a Cadillac dealer, but he may as well take over.

If one lives long enough to reach maturity, one comes to experience decline. Axel's New York job is to prepare the fish for the ocean (he makes them 'ready to die', i.e. mature). In a conversation with his Uncle Leo in the epilogue of *Arizona*, the state of maturity is described as one that comes after 'the nightmare' that separates childhood from adulthood. As a result, one reaches a different state in which, even though something new may be gained, something is irretrievably lost. Lured by those around them, maturity is the condition that Kusturica's protagonists are punished with once their coming of age is complete. They have no other choice but to put up with it, with the corruption and squalor. 'Since I started lying myself,' Perhan says, 'I do not believe anyone.'

To be mature means to know the rules of the game, to be cunning and daring, to know how to get one's own way. It means to know how to defy the rules of the game and yet make it appear fair play.

In Kusturica's universe women are eternally mature, deprived of the romantic experiences of adolescent men. Some of his secondary male characters are also mature and corrupt (Zijo in *Father*, Uncle Leo in *Arizona*, Dadan in *Black Cat*), and it is difficult to imagine what they must have been like as adolescents. As far as central characters are concerned, only three protagonists are really mature men: Meša in *Father* and Marko and Blacky in *Underground*; the equation between maturity and corruption applies to each one of them. Meša's sole corrupt feature at the opening of the film is his womanising, but as a result of the ordeal he lives through, he acquires a disparaging disposition and becomes a political opportunist and a cynic. In *Underground*, Marko is the ultimate corrupt character. Blacky, in comparison, is more simple-minded, and the fact that his level of corruption is less than Marko's only suggests his relative immaturity.

Death often comes at the brink of maturity. It happens with both Azra and Perhan in *Gypsies*, with Grace in *Arizona* and with Jovan in *Underground*. Marko's childishly simple-hearted sibling Ivan only becomes mature after killing his brother at the end of *Underground*. Immediately thereafter he commits suicide in a situation where, once again, death and maturity arrive hand in hand.

Giuseppe Ghigi talked of a certain lack of respect for death in Kusturica: while Perhan lies dead, the boy steals the gold coins from his eyes; the wedding celebration goes on even though two grandfathers die, their bodies tucked away in the attic (Boni, 1999, p. 42). The bungee-cord effect in the failing suicide attempts can also be seen as disrespectful. But it is a matter of interpretation: it may well be seen as a deliberate effort to reject death as a final experience, to provide a cheerful continuation to the life cycle. Latterly, coming back to life has become a lasting feature of Kusturica's films: Uncle Leo is alive, one more time, in the epilogue of *Arizona Dream*; everybody comes back from death to celebrate the imaginary wedding of Jovan and Jelena at the end of *Underground*; in the most inspiring scene of the film, the two old men who appeared to die during the wedding in *Black Cat* come back to life. It seems that Kusturica wants to give everyone a second chance. Resurrection is not an invitation to replay the corrupt confinement of maturity, but rather a chance to re-experience the fascination of adolescence.

In *Super 8 Stories*, Kusturica includes old home video footage that shows him playing in the snow with his five-year-old son Stribor, a little blond boy. Then there is present-day footage in which he is seen wrestling with Stribor, who has, meanwhile, grown into a bear-like twenty-year-old male. It may well be that these scenes, showing that he is still inclined to play today as if the years between make no difference, are meant to suggest that Kusturica, like his protagonists, does not want to let maturity take over. He would rather remain an adolescent and certainly wants to be taken as one.

CONCLUSION: Time of Kusturica

> In a way, my position in world cinema is not very clear: I am considered an
> auteur, which is a certain form of recognition, but it is a handicap as well.

> I do not think of myself as the new Fellini, but I believe that I continue a certain
> tradition, of the European auteurist cinema.

Kusturica, quoted in Cahiers du cinéma, 1995, p. 42

An illustrated account that can be found on Matthieu Dhennin's Kusturica
website tells of an ironic encounter documented by the French Canal+ on
11 May 1997, during the Cannes Film Festival. Strolling around Nice
airport, Emir Kusturica accidentally stumbles on Francis Ford Coppola in
the passenger waiting area. Kusturica approaches, introduces himself and
stops for a chat. Coppola, who remains seated, asks Kusturica in a friendly
way about his origins, followed by other questions from which it becomes
apparent that he is not familiar with his work. He admits to not having
seen *Underground*, and Kusturica promises to send him the film on video-
cassette.

They may both belong to that rare species of directors who have won the
Palme d'Or twice, but while it would be inconceivable for Kusturica not to
know Coppola's work, no one is really surprised that the knowledge is not
reciprocated.

The leading French directors Claude Lelouch, Jean-Marc Barr and
others have been asked for their comments on this exchange
(www.dhennin.com/kusturica). Predictably, they all point at the
metaphorical value of the episode, representing the uneasy relationship
between American and European cinema, with Kusturica standing and
Coppola sitting, an apprentice—master encounter that speaks volumes
about America's autarchic ignorance and Europe's superfluous endurance.

It is not American-sized grandeur that matters to Kusturica anyhow. His
achievement is spectacular enough in its own right. The Austrian Michael

Haneke places Kusturica's films between Shakespeare and the Marx brothers, and numerous other directors, mostly European, have made similar statements. In the cinema of the Balkans Kusturica's great international standing has provided general inspiration to many talented film-makers who feel excluded and marginalised. His imagery has been recycled in a range of new contexts, directly quoted by directors such as Serbian Srdjan Dragojevic (*Mi nismo andjeli* [*We Are No Angels*, 1992]), Bulgarian Ivan Nichev (*Sled kraya na sveta* [*After the End of the World*, 1998]) and others. Many elements in recent Russian films by leading directors, like Pavel Chukhrai's *Vor* (*Thief*, 1997), Valeriy Ogorodnikov's *Barak* (*Barracks*, 1999) and Pavel Lungin's *Svad'ba* (*The Wedding*, 2000), bear a resemblance to Kusturica's narratives and *mise-en-scènes*. The young Tadjik director Bakhtyar Khudojnazarov, an art-house favourite, used Kusturica's magical-realist devices from *Gypsies* (white veils, levitation and immaculate conception) in his Central Asia-set *Luna Papa* (*Moon Father*, 1999), a genre-defying international co-production. The lesser seen UK production *Stringer* (1998) by Polish-British Paul Pawlikowski (of *Last Resort* fame) featured a range of Kusturica references – from the youth hypnotising a rabbit (*Dolly Bell*), through the flock of geese (*Gypsies*), to the red-dressed dancer in the background (*Underground*). More parallels of this type can be found in the work of French Romani director Tony Gatlif, or with Polish magic realist Jan Jakub Kolski.

But I am inclined to see Kusturica's influence as reaching beyond the immediately detectable quotes and set-ups. The epic treatment that Kusturica gives to the simple concerns of his preferred insignificant and marginal protagonists is echoed in films that rank in the new line of controversial Cannes favourites, like Lars von Trier's *Dancer in the Dark* (2000). The intense attention that he devotes to the elaborate staging of his spectacularly overdone lavish settings is kept alive in films that claim to be the blockbusters of post-modernist art cinema, like Baz Luhrman's *Moulin Rouge* (2001).

What is even more important is that Kusturica is revered by film-makers who do not try to imitate him. Many directors who do not necessarily want their films to have the same look, dream of making movies that would have the same effect. Kusturica has set an example that will be willingly followed by all those who believe auteurism still has a chance in cinema.

BIBLIOGRAPHY

Attanasio, Paul. 'Critic's Notebook', *The Washington Post*, 6 October 1985, p. C1.

Bertellini, Giorgio. *Emir Kusturica* (Milan: Il Castoro Cinema, 1996).

——.(ed.). *Emir Kusturica*, Foreword by Lorenzo Codelli (Rome: Script/Leuto, 1995).

Bouineau, Jean-Marc. *Le petit livre de Emir Kusturica* (Garches: Spartorange, 1993).

Boni, Stefano (ed.). *Emir Kusturica* (Torino: Paravia Garage, 1999).

Burgoyne, Robert. *Film Nation: Hollywood Looks at U.S. History* (Minneapolis/London: University of Minnesota Press, 1997).

Cerović, Stanko. 'Canned Lies', 1995. Available at: http://www.barnsdle. demon.co.uk/bosnia/caned.html

Codelli, Lorenzo. 'De la colline de Kusturica: Le cinéma Yougoslave d'aujourd'hui', *Positif* 296, October 1985, pp. 12–17.

Downey, Mike L. 'Emir of Cannes', *Cinema Papers*, No. 53, September 1985, p. 13.

Feinstein, Howard. 'Above Ground: Emir Kusturica Emerges from the Furor around his Recent Hard-To-See Yugoslavian Epic', *The Village Voice*, 2 July 1996, p. 78.

Ferro, Marc. 'Conflict within the Third Man', in: *Cinema and History*, translated by Naomi Greene (Detroit: Wayne State University Press, 1988), pp. 125–32.

Finkielkraut, Alain. 'The Kusturica Imposture', in *Dispatches from the Balkan War and Other Writings*, translated by Peter S. Rogers and Richard Golsan (Lincoln: University of Nebraska Press, 1999), pp. 182–5. (Originally as 'L'imposture Kusturica', *Le Monde*, 2 June 1995).

Garbarz, Franck. 'Underground, ou l'innocence meurtrie', *Positif*, No. 417, November 1995, pp. 15–18.

Halligan, Benjamin. 'An Aesthetic of Chaos: The Blurring of Political Subtexts in Film Depictions of the Bosnian War', in Horton, A.J. (ed.). *The Celluloid Tinderbox: Yugoslav Screen Reflections of a Turbulent Decade* (London: Central Europe Review, 2000), pp. 62–89. Available at: http://www.mirhouse.com/ce-review/ Yugofilm.pdf

Handke, Peter. *A Journey to the Rivers: Justice for Serbia* (New York: Viking, 1997).

Horton, Andrew. 'Oedipus Unresolved: Covert and Overt Narrative Discourse in Emir Kusturica's *When Father Was Away on Business*', *Cinema Journal*, Vol. XXVII, No. 4, Summer 1988, pp. 64–81.

——.'Cinematic Makeovers and Cultural Border Crossings: Kusturica's *Time of the Gypsies* and Coppola's *Godfather* and *Godfather II*', in Horton, A. and Stuart V. McDougal (eds). *Play it Again, Sam: Retakes on Remakes* (Berkeley: University of California Press, 1998), pp. 172–91.

Hutcheon, Linda. *A Poetics of Postmodernism: History, Theory, Fiction* (New York and London: Routledge, 1988).

Iordanova, Dina. 'Kusturica's *Underground* (1995): Historical Allegory or Propaganda', *Historical Journal of Film, Radio and TV*, Vol. l9, No. l , l999, pp. 69–86.

——.*Cinema of Flames: Balkan Film, Culture and the Media* (London: BFI, 2001).

Kehr, Dave. 'Gypsies Defeated by Spectacle', *Chicago Tribune*, 21 February 1990, p. 7.

Krstic, Igor. 'Representing Yugoslavia? Emir Kusturica's *Underground* and the Politcis of Postmodern Cinematic Historiography', *Tijdschrift voor Mediageschiedenis. Media & Orlog* (Amsterdam), Jaargang 2, Nummer 2, December 1999, pp. 138–59.

Kusturica, Emir. 'Europe, ma ville flambe!', *Le Monde*, 24 April 1992, p. 3.

——.'Une profession de foi', translated by Svetlana Novak in Bouineau, J.-M. *Le petit livre de Emir Kusturica* (Garches: Spartorange, 1993), pp. 16–38.

——.'Mon imposture', *Le Monde*, 26 October 1995, p. 13.

——.'En bas et en haut, en haut et en bas', translated by Svetlana Novak, *Positif*, No. 417, November 1995, pp. 29–30 (Originally published 1982 in *Svjet*, Sarajevo).

——.'Souvenirs de bord', *Cahiers du cinéma*, No. 496, November 1995, pp. 42–5.

——.and Serge Grünberg (ed.). *Il était une fois… Underground* (Paris: *Cahiers du cinéma*/CiBY 2000, 1995).

Levi, Pavle. 'From *When Father Was Away on Business* to *Underground*: Emir

Kusturica's Aesthetic of the Gentrifugal Libido', talk at SCS annual conference, Washington, DC, May 2001.

Lyotard, Jean-François. *The Post Modern Condition: a Report on Knowledge*, translated by Geoff Bennington and Brian Massumi (Manchester: Manchester University Press, 1981).

Malcolm, Derek. 'The Surreal Sarajevan Dreamer', *The Guardian*, 29 June 1995, p. 10.

Mars-Jones, Adam. 'Vision improbable: Serbian film-maker Emir Kusturica's elephantine comedy lays claim to the high ground of European art cinema', *The Independent*, 7 March 1996, p. 7.

Maslin, Janet. '*Arizona Dream*: Lunacy With Missing Minutes', *New York Times*, 7 June 1995, Section C, p. 13.

Orr, John. *The Art and Politics of Film* (Edinburgh: Edinburgh University Press, 2000).

Ostria, Vincent. 'Monsieur K. a Prague', *Cahiers du cinéma*, No. 481, June 1994, pp. 72–82.

——.'Papa est en voyage d'affairs', *Avant-Scene* (Special Issue), No. 447, December 1995, pp. 1–84.

Rayns, Tony. '*Underground*', *Sight and Sound*, March 1996, pp. 53–4.

Romney, Jonathan. 'Slav labour', *The New Statesman*, Vol. 12, No. 554, 10 May 1999, pp. 34–5. Available at: http://www.newstatesman.co.uk/ 199905100034.htm

Rosenstone, Robert A. 'The Future of the Past: Film and the Beginnings of Postmodern History', in Sobchack, Vivian (ed.). *The Persistence of History: Cinema, Television and the Modern Event*

(London and New York: Routledge,
1998), pp. 201–19.

Taylor, Richard, Julian Graffy, Nancy Wood
and Dina Iordanova (eds). *BFI
Companion to Eastern European and
Russian Cinema* (London: BFI, 2000).
Entries on Emir Kusturica, Yugoslavia,
Yugoslavia's Break-Up in Film, Goran
Bregović, Dušan Kovačević, Miki
Manojlović.

Vecchi, Paolo. *Emir Kusturica* (Rome:
Gremese Editore, 1999).

White, Hayden. 'The Modernist Event', in
Sobchack, Vivian (ed.). *The Persistence of
History: Cinema, Television and the Modern
Event* (London and New York: Routledge,
1997), pp. 17–39.

Wilmington, Michael. '*Black Cat, White Cat*'
is a Crazy Delight', *Chicago Tribune*,
22 October 1999, p. A/CN.

Yarovskaya, Marianna. '*Underground*', *Film
Quarterly* 51, No. 2, Winter 1997–98,
pp. 50–54.

Žižek, Slavoj. 'You May', *London Review of
Books*, Vol. 21, No. 6, 18 March 1999.
Available at: http:www.lrb.co.uk/
v21/no6/zize2106.htm

Selected interviews
(in chronological order)

'Entretien avec Emir Kusturica', interview
with Lorenzo Codelli, *Positif* 296,
October 1985, pp. 18–22.

'Winner from the Balkans', interview with
Henry Kamm, *New York Times*, 24
November 1985, Section 2, p. 21.

'Entre ciel et terre', interview with Iannis
Katsahnias, *Cahiers du cinéma*, No. 425,
1989, pp. 37–8.

'Entretien avec Emir Kusturica', interview
with Michel Ciment and Lorenzo
Codelli, *Positif* 345, November 1989,
pp. 4–8.

'Entering the Oscar Race Via Magic and
Realism', interview with Kevin Thomas,
Los Angeles Times, 9 February 1990, Part
F, p. 6.

'La quête du pays uncertain', interview with
Michel Beauchamp and Gérard Grugeau,
24 Images, No. 49, Summer 1990,
pp. 57–9.

'A Bosnian Movie-Maker Laments the
Death of the Yugoslav Nation', interview
with David Binder, *New York Times*,
25 October 1992, Section 4, p. 7.

'Les films doivent être plus grands que la
vie', interview with Daniele Heymann
and Jean-Michel Frodon, *Le Monde*,
6 January 1993, p. 15.

'Comment "voler" le film', interview with
Michel Ciment, *Positif*, No. 383, January
1993, pp. 20–25.

'Conversation secrete', interview with Jean-
Marc Bouineau, 25 February – 6 March
1993, in Bouineau, J.-M. *Le petit livre de
Emir Kusturica*, pp. 44–78.

'Le vol du flétan', interview with Philippe
Elhem, *24 Images*, No. 66, April–May
1993, pp. 19–23.

'Die Wüste ist der Ort der Poesie', interview
with Fritz Göttler, *Süddeutsche Zeitung*,
13 May 1993.

'Propos de Emir Kusturica', interview with
Thierry Jousse and Serge Grünberg,
Cahiers du cinéma, No. 492, June 1995,
pp. 69–71.

'Aujourd'hui, plus que jamais, le réalisme
m'ennuie', interview with Michel

Ciment, *Positif*, No. 417, November
   1995, pp. 22–7.
'In der Falle der Geschichte', interview with
   H. G. Pflaum, *Süddeutsche Zeitung*,
   23 November 1995, p. 16.
'Verzichtsgelübde & Magengeschwüre',
   interview with Harald Pauli, *Focus*,
   21 December 1996, No. 52,
   pp. 134–6.
'Les couleurs, la texture, l'espace, les
   sentiments profonds …', interview with
   Michel Ciment, *Positif*, No. 452, August
   1998, pp. 19–23.
'Incontro con il regista', transcript Sandra
   Campanini from a discussion held on 6
   February 1999 in Teatro Valli di Reggio
   Emilia, in Boni, S.(ed.). *Emir Kusturica*,
   pp. 20–26.
'He Duels, He Brawls, He Helps Cows to
   Give Birth … And He Makes Films',
   interview with Fiachra Gibbons, *The
   Guardian*, 23 April 1999, Friday Review
   – G2, pp.1–3. Available at:
   http://film.guardian.co.uk/Feature_Stor
   y/Guardian/0,,44289,00.html
'The Director They Couldn't Quash: Emir
   Kusturica', interview with Graham
   Fuller, *Interview*, Vol. 29, No. 9, 1
   September 1999, pp. 68–71.
'Enough Retirement! Kusturica Returns to
   Gypsy Life', interview with Howard

Feinstein, *New York Times*, 5 September
   1999, Section 2, p. 7.
'Momentum and Emotion', interview
   with Anthony Kaufman, *Indie Wire*,
   7 September 1999. Available at:
   http://www.indiewire.com/film/inter-
   views/int Kusturica Emir 990909.html
'Čovjek bez pobune nije ćovjek', interview
   with Jasmina Lekic, *NIN*, No. 2618,
   1 March 2001. Available at:
   http://www.nin.co.yu/2001-03/
   01/16842.html

Documentaries

Shooting Days (Czechoslovakia, Aleksandar
   Manic, 1997)
South Bank Show: Emir Kusturica (UK, Gerald
   Fox, 2000)

Websites

Matthieu Dhennin's Emir Kusturica (1998).
   Available at:
   http://www.dhennin.com/kusturica
Komuna (1998) Available at:
   http://www.komuna.co.yu
Emir Kusturica and the No Smoking Orchestra
   (2000) Available at:
   http://www.emirkusturica-
   nosmoking.com

FILMOGRAPHY

Dio istine
(*Part of the Truth*, 1971)
Black and White

Jesen (*Autumn*, 1972)
Black and White

Guernica (1977)
Screenplay: Pavel Sykora, Emir Kusturica,
   based on a story by Antonije Isaković
Editor: Borek Lipský, Peter Beovsky
Production: FAMU Prague
Running time: 25 minutes
Black and White

Nevjeste dolaze
(*The Brides Are Coming*, 1978)
Screenplay: Ivica Matić
Director of Photography: Vilko Filač
Music: Zoran Simjanović
Selected cast: Milka Kokotović-Podrug,
   Miodrag Krstović, Bogdan Diklić
Production: Televizija Sarajevo
Running time: 73 minutes
Colour

Bife Titanik (*Bar Titanic*, 1979)
Screenplay: Ján Beran, Emir Kusturica,
   based on the story by Ivo Andrić
Editor: Ruža Cvingl
Director of Photography: Vilko Filač
Music: Zoran Simjanović
Selected cast: Boro Stjepanović,
   Bogdan Diklić

Production: Televizija Sarajevo
Running time: 62 minutes
Colour

Sjećaš li se Dolly Bell?
(*Do You Remember Dolly Bell?*,
1981)
Screenplay: Abdulah Sidran with Emir
   Kusturica, based on Sidran's novel
Editor: Senija Tičić
Director of Photography: Vilko Filač
Music: Zoran Simjanović
Selected cast: Slavko Štimac,
   Slobodan Aligrudić, Pavle Vujišić
Production: Sutjeska Film, Televizija Sarajevo
Distribution: International Home Cinema
   (USA)
Running time: 108 minutes
Colour

Otac na službenom putu
(*When Father Was Away on
Business*, 1985)
Screenplay: Abdulah Sidran based on his novel
Editor: Andrija Zafranović
Director of Photography: Vilko Filač
Music: Zoran Simjanović
Selected cast: Moreno Debartoli,
   Miki Manojlović, Mirjana Karanović,
   Mira Furlan, Davor Dujmović,
   Mustafa Nadarević, Pavle Vujišić
Production: Forum Film
Distribution: Cannon Films (USA)
Running time: 135 minutes
Colour

Dom za vešanje (*Time of the Gypsies*, 1989)

Screenplay: Emir Kusturica, Gordan Mihić
Editor: Andrija Zafranović
Director of Photography: Vilko Filač
Production designer: Miljen Kljaković 'Kreka'
Sound: Ivan Zakić
Music: Goran Bergović
Consultant: Rajko Djurić
Selected cast: Davor Dujmović,
    Ljubica Adžović, Bora Todorović,
    Sinolička Trpkova
Production: Forum Film, Televizija
    Sarajevo, Smart Egg Pictures (London)
Distribution: Columbia Pictures (USA)
Running time: 138 minutes
Colour

Arizona Dream (1993)

Screenplay: David Atkins
Story: Emir Kusturica, David Atkins
Editor: Andrija Zafranović
Director of Photography: Vilko Filač
Production designer:
    Miljen Kljaković 'Kreka'
Sound: Vincent Arnardi
Music: Goran Bergović
Songs performed by Iggy Pop
Selected cast: Johnny Depp,
    Faye Dunaway, Jerry Lewis,
    Lili Taylor, Vincent Gallo
Executive producer: Paul R. Gurian
Producer: Claudie Ossard
Co-producer: Richard Brick
Production: Constellation, UGC, Hachette
    Première, with the participation of Canal+
Distribution: Warner Bros (USA), Electric
    Pictures (UK)
Running time: 136 minutes
Colour

Underground/*Once Upon a Time There Was a Country* (*Podzemlje: Bila jednom jedna zemlja*, 1995)

Screenplay: Dušan Kovačević and Emir
    Kusturica, based on motifs of Kovačević's
    plays
Editor: Branka Čeperac
Director of Photography: Vilko Filač
Production designer:
    Miljen Kljaković 'Kreka'
Sound: Marko Rodić
Sound editor: Svetolik-Mića Zajc
Music: Goran Bergović
Selected cast: Miki Manojlović,
    Lazar Ristovski, Mirjana Joković,
    Srdjan Todorović, Slavko Štimac,
    Davor Dujmović, Mirjana Karanović
Executive producer: Pierre Spengler
Producers: Maksa Catović,
    Karl Baumgartner
Production: CiBY 2000 (Paris), Pandora
    Film (Frankfurt), Novo Film (Budapest).
    In collaboration with Komuna and RTS
    (Radio-Television Serbia), Yugoslavia;
    Mediarex/Etic, Czech Republic;
    Tchapline Films, Bulgaria
Financial support: Film Fund Hamburg and
    Eurimages
Distribution: New Yorker Films (USA),
    Artificial Eye (UK), Komuna (Yugoslavia)
Running time: 167 minutes
Colour.

Crna mačka, beli mačor
(Black Cat, White Cat, 1998)

Screenplay: Gordan Mihić
Editor: Svetolik-Mića Zajc
Director of Photography: Thierry Arbogast
Additional photography: Michel Amathieu
Sound: Nenad Vukadinović
Music: Dr Nele Karajilić, Vojislav Aralica,
    Dejan Sparavalo
Selected cast: Bajram Severdžan,
    Srdjan Todorović, Branka Katić,
    Florijan Ajdini, Ljubica Adžović
Executive producer: Maksa Catović
Production: CiBY 2000 (Paris),
    Pandora Film (Frankfurt),
    Komuna (Belgrade)
Distribution: USA Films (USA),
    Komuna (Yugoslavia), Artificial Eye (UK)
Running time: 130 minutes
Colour

Super 8 Stories (2001)

Editor: Svetolik-Mića Zajc
Director of Photography: Michel Amathieu,
    Chico De Luigi, Petar Popović,
    Gianenrico 'Gogo' Bianchi, Gerd Breiter,
    Frédéric Burgue, Pascal Caubère,
    Raimond Goebel, Thorsten Königs,
    Ratko Kušić, Emir Kusturica,
    Dragan Radivojević Lav,
    Stephan Schmidt, Darko Vučić
Sound designer: Svetolik-Mića Zajc
Music: No Smoking Orchestra
Production: Fandango, Pandora
    Filmproduktion GmbH
Distribution: Orfeo Films International,
    BFI Programme Unit/ICA Cinema (UK)
Running time: 90 minutes
Black and White/Colour.

INDEX

Bold type denotes detailed analysis of a film; italics denote illustrations